Second Edition

# WHATEVER IT TAKES
## The Realities
## of Managerial
## Decision Making

### Morgan W. McCall, Jr.
*University of Southern California*

### Robert E. Kaplan
*Center for Creative Leadership,*
*Greensboro, N.C.*

Prentice Hall, Upper Saddle River, New Jersey 07458

*Library of Congress Cataloging-in-Publication Data*

McCall, Morgan W.
    Whatever it takes: the realities of managerial decision making /
Morgan W. McCall, Jr., Robert E. Kaplan.—2nd ed.
      p. cm.
    ISBN 0-13-952136-4
    1. Decision-making.  I. Kaplan, Robert E. II.  Title.
HD30.23.M39    1990
658.4'03—dc20      89-38042

Editorial/production supervision: *Edith Riker/Bea Marcks*
Cover design: George Cornell
Manufacturing buyer: *Ed O'Dougherty*

Previously published as: *Whatever It
Takes: Decision Makers at Work*

 © 1990 by Prentice-Hall, Inc.
A Simon & Schuster Company
Upper Saddle River, New Jersey 07458

Printed in the United States of America

10 9 8 7

ISBN    0-13-952136-4

Prentice-Hall International (UK) Limited, *London*
Prentice-Hall of Australia Pty. Limited, *Sydney*
Prentice-Hall Canada Inc., *Toronto*
Prentice-Hall Hispanoamericana, S.A., *Mexico*
Prentice-Hall of India Private Limited, *New Delhi*
Prentice-Hall of Japan, Inc., *Tokyo*
Simon & Schuster Asia Ptc. Ltd., *Singapore*
Editora Prentice-Hall do Brasil. Ltda., *Rio de Janeiro*

Dedicated to our parents, without whom
none of this would have been possible:

Morgan and Ada Belle McCall

Harry and Lillian Kaplan

# CONTENTS

# FOREWORD

Many scholars have recognized that decision making comes close to being—if it is not in fact—the very heart of managerial work. Managers are deluged with choices, options, and information, good and bad. Saddled with heavy demands on their time, with resources that are not always adequate to their responsibilities, and with unrealistic expectations on the part of superiors (or shareholders and financial institutions), they must pick and choose an action route around both buried antipersonnel mines and highly visible obstacles.

Students of business have reacted to the preeminence of decision making with a wealth of studies that extend from the pioneering work by the Carnegie-Mellon "school" of Herbert Simon and his disciples to a continuous stream of work by economists and psychologists of many persuasions. Regrettably, many of these treated decision making as though it were the product of a somewhat rational individual executive (who might satisfice when he or she couldn't quite maximize) or of a struggling small group confronting a problem and a time clock. The usual surrogates for both of these were typically eager students solving contrived problems behind one-way mirrors.

At long last two distinguished management researchers have taken decision making out of the laboratory "closet" (more fairly "test room") and set it where it properly deserves to be. They have provided a rich, realistic, and useful analysis of the problems of decision making in *organizations,* in real, live, breathing complex organizations—very different from isolated individuals doing their calculus of pain and pleasure or small groups playing games.

Though it is easy to say that a good organization is one that has made good decisions, the big question is *how* to make good decisions. Insisting on rationality (as opposed to emotionality) and on facts, logic, and common sense is not enough. Everyone subscribes, but few pay their bills.

McCall and Kaplan very properly recognize that the decision itself is merely the tip of the proverbial iceberg. Long before a hard choice is made, managers must decide what to look for and what to look at. This reminds us of what historians have told us for eons: History isn't the account of all that happened, but the reconstruction of what someone decides is significant. And, so it is with the typical manager who, with countless things to attend to, must, as the authors point out, have the special skills to know *how* to look, *where* to look, and *when* to look.

And, if that were not problematic enough, we also know that, except in detective stories, the facts don't speak for themselves; they must be interpreted. But there is more; after interpretation, managers must still evaluate what do about these facts, whether they represent problems or opportunities. The art of successful management is, in part, knowing when to act and when not; and it is knowing how to act: when to confront and when to negotiate, or modify, or mollify.

While they don't neglect the individual's blinders and distortions—the impact of "mental maps" and values and sensitivities—McCall and Kaplan give a superb account of the ways in which organizational forces such as hierarchical controls and socialization shape and misshape decision making.

An organization or an individual seeking to improve the quality of decision making should find this volume of great value because it works at many levels. It is a flesh, straightforward, "unjargoned" description of what decision making is really like in modern organizations. Without pretentions or cumbersomeness it introduces the reader to the more important concepts of both organization theory and decision theory as they apply to managing decisions. And it is concerned with moving from what is to what could be; namely improvement. All in all, it is a most valid and useful work on a subject that is not new but is rarely treated so soundly.

*Leonard R. Sayles*

# ACKNOWLEDGMENTS

The writing of this book has been no less convoluted than many of the managerial decisions we have described. As we wended our way down the circuitous path, many people made valuable contributions. At the top of the list is Bill Drath, who helped us overcome writer's block and brought some semblance of logic to the organization of the manuscript.

Also at the top of the list are the many managers and executives who gave their time and insights. Their experiences and craftsmanship, their pain and joy, inspired this book in the first place and are at the heart of what we describe. While there isn't space to thank each of them by name, Gene Cattabiani, Lou Kaplan, Linda Kaplan, Roger Kelley, Jim Bruce, and Roger Anthony deserve special mention for the *many* hours they spent opening our eyes to the realities of managers at work.

This manuscript benefited greatly from the comments of our colleagues. Dave Brown, Terry Connolly, David DeVries, Mike Lombardo, Steve Wall, Steve Stumpf, Vanya Orlans, Jim Waters, and Milton Blood, among others, all offered sage counsel.

Creating a physical manuscript is no small feat, and we are immensely grateful to Alice Warren, Joanne Ferguson, and Mid Dohm for the many hours they put in. Frank Freeman and Karen Barden not only tracked down many references but also slogged through the creation of the index. By the time of the second edition, Alice Warren had become a research assistant and helped with the literature review as well as with an overall reading of the book.

Special thanks go to David Hills who brought his wit to the illustrations in this book. Thanks, too, to Michael Gerlach, who coauthored with us the technical report from whence this book sprang.

Finally, Biscuitville on Market Street in Greensboro deserves the patience award for tolerating Bob Kaplan's endless hours writing in the back booth.

On a serious note, we want to recognize our special debt to an executive who spent many patient hours with us sharing his experiences and insights about management and the decision-making process. When Morgan W. McCall, Sr., died last fall, the world of management lost a good executive and the world of research lost a valuable resource. We'll miss him.

# CREDITS

The authors would like to thank the proprietors for permission to quote from copyrighted works, as follows:

# PREFACE

The first step in doing a revision is bringing together various reviews of the first edition. Until that time authors can delude themselves about how successfully they achieved their original goals. Therefore, we were pleased that the reviews of *Whatever It Takes,* while chock-full of useful suggestions, described what we had hoped to write: a book thoroughly grounded in research, supplemented by the experiences of executives and managers, written in an entertaining and readable way that would paint a realistic picture of what managers were up against "out there." In fact, a concern of several critics was that we would ruin what we had done by messing with it.

Preserving the original's approach, style, audience, and intent was our major priority for the second edition. Rather than undertaking a massive overhaul, we opted for a more modest updating and elaboration. We fleshed out some content areas that readers felt deserved more attention. We reviewed the research that had accumulated since 1984 and incorporated what we could into the book. We asked our artist, David Hills, to consider some new cartoons.

What we offer here is meant to bring to life the dilemmas of decision making on line, where the best advice to managers who want to make effective decisions is still to "do whatever it takes." In the intervening years since the first edition, no one has found the Rosetta stone of decisions. No fancy algorithms were derived that solve our major problems, and no one found a way to replace experience as the managerial teacher. Research on decision making has proceeded apace, and each year adds substantially to our knowledge. Great strides have been made in some areas like artificial intelligence, which is revolutionizing the ways computers work.

But when it comes to human beings making decisions in organizations, the world is, if anything, even more complex, more ambiguous, more difficult than it was a few years ago. If anything, the pace of change continues to accelerate. Managers still have to make decisions on ill-defined issues, without all the information they need, in a context of competing pressures. The trivial and the titanic still tumble out capriciously, showing no respect for anyone's plans or priorities. While we have gotten quite good at programming computers to play chess with us, we still fumble around when it comes to deciding how to cut costs while improving service and calming irate customers.

So we hope the perspective we have tried to provide is timely and useful in the trenches, where absolutes are hard to trust and pragmatic advice is hard to find. We still offer what we think is useful from those who have done research and those who have fought the battles. And, lest any of us take ourselves too seriously, we still leaven this analysis with humor.

Since the first edition was written, both of us have experienced firsthand and in some depth the challenges of managing. Neither succeeded fully in following our own advice. Both of us, however, have emerged with an even deeper respect for the managers and executives out there with the courage and ability to make the decisions on which our organizations depend. In this age of highly publicized greed and corruption, we sometimes forget that the vast majority of us are doing the best we can with what we've got. And many do an exceptional job at a difficult business. We salute the managers who care and dare to try. We hope this second edition offers some ideas that will help them do just a little bit better and feel a little better about what they do.

# PREFACE

# TO THE FIRST EDITION

Our perceptions of organizational decision-making . . . tend to emphasize the *product* of decision-making—never (or rarely) the *process*. Those elements of chance, ignorance, stupidity, recklessness, and amiable confusion are simply not reckoned with. They are selectively ignored, it seems. Thus, the public rarely sees the hundreds of small tableaux, the little dramas, that result in a policy statement or a bit of strategy. It sees only the move or hears only the statement, and it not unreasonably assumes that such an action is the result of a dispassionate, almost mechanical process in which problems are perceived, alternative solutions weighed, and rational decisions made.[1]

[Being a manager is] a lot of fun if you are with people who are supportive, and you have the right kind of financial backing to go ahead with these projects, and if you know what you're doing. (president of a small company)

Our initial intent was to review research on decision making with implications for understanding what managers are up to in organizations. As we began gathering articles, it quickly became apparent that the quantity of material on decision making far exceeds what could be reviewed or even read for a book like this. There are literally thousands of studies available, not to mention the formidable collection of advice for decision makers. Many different disciplines have had a crack at the topic: economics, political science, public policy, management science, and various branches of psychology—to mention only a few. Different aspects or pieces of the decision process have received attention, including information processing, choice, participation, deciding how to decide and so forth. Different methods have been used, ranging from laboratory experiments to protocol analysis to interviews to case studies.

In all this bewildering array, we were struck by the absence of research confronting head-on the messiness and complexity of decision making as it unfolds in organizations. Further, some aspects of the process were virtually untouched. Little could be found on how managers identify problems in the first place, or why they choose to work on some problems rather than others, or how decisions get made in the discontinuous, fragmented, chaotic world of a manager handling many problems at the same time.

Almost in desperation, then, we latched onto a dozen or so studies that had been done in the field with actual decision makers making decisions that counted for something. We used this core to frame the managerial decision process and then tried to add in the vast array of other research and historical accounts were they seemed to clarify or elaborate on something managers did. As the framework took shape, we asked a number of executives and managers to review it for us and tell us if it made any sense. We also took advantage of several work-shops to test our concepts with managers and to collect firsthand accounts of managerial problem-solving situations. Most important of all, we contacted a dozen or so managers and executives we had reason to believe were particularly effective decision makers. We interviewed them intensively about the problems they face, how they identify them, and what they do about them.

What resulted was not the comprehensive review of the literature we had originally contemplated, but rather a focused and sometimes speculative discussion of what managers seem to be doing in their day-to-day involvement with decisions.

## DECISION-MAKING THEORY, CLASSICAL AND CURRENT

In the face of the nigh-overwhelming complexity and changeability of the manager's world, management theorists have attempted to define away some of the intractability and thereby reduce the manager's job to manageable proportions. Classical theorists offered what Connolly termed "the proper decision-making sequence": careful definition of the problem, an exhaustive search for information, generation of numerous alterna-

tives, and a calculated choice among the alternatives.[2] As Burns put it, "classical thinking about executive decision making has viewed the process as an essentially orderly and rational one. A problem is defined and isolated; information is gathered; alternatives are set forth; an end is established; means are created to achieve the end; a choice is made."[3] John Dewey is often credited with formulating this systematic approach to tackling problems. And structure, even for the most unstructured problems, is needed and appreciated. The trouble comes when the attempt to tame unruly problems is carried too far, when our prescriptions are too simple to account for the realities of managerial problem solving.

Managerial decision making is rarely a matter of picking up a single problem and disposing of it in expeditious step-by-step fashion. With every problem comes a context, which includes its own history and the host of related and unrelated problems that coexist with it. "Executive decision making is not a series of single linear acts like baking a pie. It is a process, a sequence of behavior, that stretches back into a murky past and forward into a murkier future. [It is] a turbulent stream rather than . . . an assembly-line operation . . . a twisted, unshapely halting flow."[4] The laboratory research on human judgment (decision making) has been limited largely to discrete choices taken in isolation and has given short shrift to the "continuous, adaptive nature of the judgmental processes used to cope with a complex, changing environment."[5] Likewise, the concept of decision making found in western countries emphasizes problems taken out at a time and solved once and for all. This is in contrast to "the Eastern philosophical traditions [which emphasize] individual accommodation to a continuously unfolding set of events."[6] This book is about decision making and problem solving in context, as the entire interconnected array plays out over time.

## THE CONTEXT OF MANAGERIAL
## DECISION MAKING

Much of the interest in decision making appears to stem from the fallibility of the human decision maker. Things that go awry seem to hold attention longer than things that go smoothly. A lot has been written on the limits of human information processing ability and the numberless personal motives that affect individual choice in spite of the facts. We want to be clear from the start that it is not our intent to condemn managers for their faults. In fact, there are so many reasons that decision making can go wrong, it's amazing how well most organizations actually do. We believe that it is the nature of the managerial job, not simply the limited capacity of individuals, that makes managerial decision making so complex and often so difficult to comprehend.

What is the context in which managers make decisions? One of the most articulate spokesmen on the subject is Leonard Sayles, and the following excerpts give the flavor of what we are dealing with:

- most problems are not solved but only "contained"
- distractions are the reality

- management . . . is dealing with the unexpected that interferes with expectations
- [it is a] never-ending series of contacts with other people
- the pace is fast, pressured, and demanding
- there are no "production functions" for most important questions.[7]

It is, in short, a job where information is transmitted mostly orally and often in fragments; where there is always more than one problem in need of attention; where other people with different values and interests are almost always involved; and where there is seldom enough time to devote to any one issue. These characteristics sharply demarcate *managerial* from other kinds of decision making, such as deciding on the next move in a game of chess or investigating a single problem over an extended period of time. These characteristics also muddy the classic distinction between "problem solving" and "decision making," and we will not make such a distinction here. For managers, problem solving and decision making are part and parcel of the same thing, and what is needed is a new term to encompass both. While waiting for a poet to find the new word, we have used problem solving and decision making interchangeably throughout the book.

## A ROAD MAP TO THE BOOK

Our goal in this book was to use research on decision making to understand how managers in organizational settings go about making decisions. Because decision making in organizations is a complex process that is hard to observe[8] and because the process seldom has clear stages that can be discussed as discrete entities, we sought to organize the research to reflect these characteristics. We were only partially successful. After the introductory section, the book is organized as if decision making unfolds in a chronological sequence from recognition of a problem to its resolution. This is clearly not the case. Instead, decisions are made and problems solved in fits and starts. The process is like a flowing stream, filled with debris, meandering through the terrain of managers and their organizations. There is no clear beginning or end. This is the message of Chapter 1.

Chapter 2 of this book deals with recognition of problematic situations. Just how is it that jumbles of facts and events get interpreted as problems in the torrent of information and situations? The ways managers interpret these streams, punctuate the reality,[9] is a key to understanding why and which problems get recognized. Organizational structure and procedures are intended to channel these streams to and through managers, sometimes providing at least a partial problem definition in the process. Other problems, and especially opportunities, may not flow through structures, and structures often carry problems and events to the wrong places.

Chapter 3 tackles the issue of why some problems get worked on and others are ignored. Just how is it that managers, aware of many problems that need attention, set priorities? There is more than enough going on to keep managers busy all day. Awareness that problematic situations exist is insufficient to guarantee doing anything about them. The manager's day is highly fragmented, full of brief episodes on a myriad of issues, overloaded with information, largely oral and interactive, current-focused, and filled with a capricious interspersion of the mundane and the significant.[10]

Attacking problems is often a messy business. Identification, definition, discovery of alternatives, evaluation, and sometimes choice can

occur simultaneously, or vaguely, or not at all. "Muddling through," "groping brick by brick" may be generous descriptions of what actually happens. Chapter 4 examines problem-solving cycles by looking at what happens to problems that attract someone's attention. Some problems get immediate action while others go through a complex, convoluted decision process.

Chapter 5 looks at what happens after decisions get made, at how they cling together or silently slip away. Many problems never really get solved, they just get held off a little longer. They tend to reappear in altered forms at another time or another place. It is often hard to know what happened, and sometimes managers don't even know that a decision was made. Choices often return to the stream, only to create new problems for someone else, to lie dormant and reappear later, or to evolve to a new stage altogether. Patterns in streams of decisions have been described as strategy,[11] reflecting that fragments returning to the stream have a larger existence either by accident or design. (See Figure P-1 for display of the major elements of the book.)

Finally, Chapter 6 outlines some implications for managers, organizations, training, and research. It suggests that thinking of decision making as an orderly, logical process, then training managers to do it that way, is not likely to make much difference.

In general, the book is intended to accomplish two purposes, which may on the face of it seem to conflict. The first purpose is to show what managers are up against as they move through the crowded and shifting vistas of problems, people, pressures, and resources. The second purpose is to suggest rules of thumb for managers to use as they attempt to find direction and achieve movement. In our effort to offer something pragmatic, we draw on the experience of veteran managers, who address the reader in their own words. Our goal is to do justice to the stiff challenges inherent in taking managerial action and at the same time to provide a modicum of guidance for taking effective action.

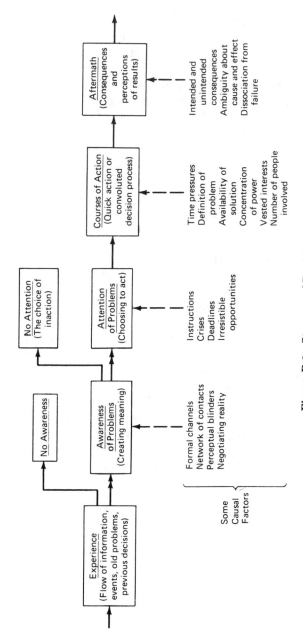

**Figure P-1  Streams of Decisions**

# 1

# *THEY HAVE SOWN THE WIND*

# *AND*

# *THEY SHALL REAP THE*

# *WHIRLWIND*

A klaxon goes off. Plus nine seconds.

> BERKOZ: "What happened?"
> ULUSMAN: "The cabin blew out."

Eleven seconds.

> BERKOZ: "Are you sure?"

Sixteen seconds.

> BERKOZ: "Bring it up. Pull her nose up."
> ULUSMAN: "I can't bring it up—she doesn't respond."

Twenty-three seconds.

> AN UNIDENTIFIED VOICE: "Nothing is left."
> ANOTHER VOICE: "Seven thousand feet."

Klaxon sounds, warning that the plane has gone over the "never-exceed" speed. Thirty-two seconds.

| | |
|---|---|
| BERKOZ: | "Hydraulics?" |
| ANOTHER VOICE: | "We have lost it . . . oops, oops." |

Fifty-four seconds.

| | |
|---|---|
| BERKOZ: | "It looks like we are going to hit the ground." |

Fifty-six seconds.

| | |
|---|---|
| BERKOZ: | "Speed." |

Sixty-one seconds.

| | |
|---|---|
| BERKOZ: | "Oops." |

Seventy-seven seconds. Sound of initial impact.

The flight recorder suggests that during the last few seconds Berkoz or Ulusman juggled with the throttles in an attempt to raise the airplane's nose and then shut off all power. The DC-10 did level out of its dive and was almost horizontal when it reached the roof of the forest.
Ship 29 hit the ground at 497 miles an hour.[1]

This grisly transcript records the last seventy-seven seconds of a Turkish Airlines DC-10 that, on March 3, 1974, crashed into the Forest of Ermenonville outside Paris. A cargo door came open in flight causing the collapse of the cabin floor, which in turn severed most of the major control systems and backup systems in the aircraft. Three hundred forty-six passengers and crew members died that day in what was at the time the largest single aircraft toll ever.

The seventy-seven seconds of dialogue listed above represent the ultimate example of decision making under stress. When the door of the aircraft came off, pilots Berkoz and Ulusman must have been confronted with a Christmas tree of warning lights and buzzers telling them of the dozens of non-operative systems. In those seconds, they had to diagnose what had happened and what could be done, all while their plane lurched out of control.

To understand why this accident took place, three journalists attempted to piece together the events leading up to it. They found that explaining this crash required them to trace the history of the aviation industry. The crash involved a string of decisions made on many levels, including entry into the wide-body airplane competition, strategies for beating competitors to the marketplace, ignoring safety data on the cargo door, making concessions on overseas sales, and inadequate training of ground crews—to mention only a few. The researchers never could identify any one decision maker as the culprit.[2]

The point is that decisions—even those that on the surface seem straightforward, such as the design of a cargo door latch—are not simple, discrete events. In this case, hundreds of people were involved, hundreds of decisions were made, many different organizations participated, vast quantities of information were processed, massive external forces came into play, and it took a long time for the accumulated decisions to have their dramatic impact. To talk of decision making in an organizational context is to talk of this complexity, to address *streams of decisions* that flow through many people and to destinations often unpredicted. It is safe to say that no one involved with the DC-10 wanted that crash to happen, yet at some point previous decisions made it almost inevitable. Many of the key decisions were made long before there was a DC-10, much less a risky door. The results cannot be blamed on stupidity or malice alone.

The streams of decisions in an organizational context are more complicated than the example of the DC-10. Take, for example, Winston Churchill's description of the decision to use the atomic bomb on Japan:

> At any rate, there never was a moment's discussion as to whether the atomic bomb should be used or not. To avert a vast, indefinite butchery, to bring the war to an end, to give peace to the world, to lay healing hands upon its tortured peoples by a manifestation of overwhelming power at the cost of a few explosions, seemed, after all our toils and perils, a miracle of deliverance.
>
> . . . The final decision now lay in the main with President Truman, who had the weapon; but I never doubted what it would be, nor have I ever doubted since that he was right. The historic fact remains, and must be judged in the after-time, that the decision whether or not to use the atomic bomb to compel the surrender of Japan was never even an issue. There was unanimous, automatic, unquestioned agreement around our table; nor did I ever hear the slightest suggestion that we should do otherwise.[3]

Sometimes, what in retrospect appears to be the major issue—in this case a decision on whether to use a highly lethal and largely untested bomb or to finish off the already reeling Japanese by conventional methods—is never a question. For the decision makers at the time, the tougher issue was when and how much to tell the Russians. The context at the time the decision was made, at least as Churchill described it, was critical to understanding the decision and, more particularly, to understanding the way the problem was defined.

As this example shows, even decisions of huge magnitude may not appear to be made in an orderly, logical, rational fashion. So much depends on how the problem is defined—To end the war quickly? To save civilian lives? To protect the secret weapon?—an issue dependent in large part on how information and situations are put together against the backdrop of events by the decision makers involved. In short, it makes little sense to focus exclusively on a choice when the definition of the problem itself can easily predetermine choice. And, as was clearly the case in the decision to use the bomb, choices create new arrays of problems.

An example of how a series of previous decisions can affect subsequent problem definition and choice comes from Dixon's description of the decisions involved with the Allied attack through Holland in 1944. After the decision to launch the operation had been made, logistical and strategic issues debated and settled, political implications battled through, and the literal wheels set in motion, new information entered the system:

> The whole enterprise depended upon an absence of strong German forces both in the Arnhem area and on the approach route from the south. Hence it came as something of a jolt when SHAEF received reports from the Dutch underground that two S.S. Panzer divisions which had mysteriously "disappeared" some time previously had now reappeared almost alongside the dropping zone. . . .
>
> This was the moment to reassess the risks involved. But since these ugly facts did not accord with what had been planned they fell upon a succession of deaf ears. Taking a lead from Montgomery, who had described the SHAEF report as ridiculous, British 2nd Army Headquarters were quick to discount it also. When one of his intelligence officers showed him the aerial photographs of German armour, General Browning, at First British Airborne H.Q., retorted: "I wouldn't trouble myself about these if I were you . . . they're probably not serviceable at any rate." The intelligence officer was then visited by the Corps medical officer, who suggested he should take some leave because he was so obviously exhausted. And at First Allied Army H.Q. the Chief Intelligence Officer, a British lieutenant-colonel, decided there was no direct evidence that the Arnhem area contained "much more than the considerable flak defenses already known to exist." As Ryan puts it: "All down the Allied line of command the evaluation of intelligence on the Panzers in the Arnhem area was magnificently bungled."
>
> Finally, just in case there were any residual doubts, the intelligence staff of the 2nd Army came up with the reassuring opinion that any German forces in the Arnhem area were "weak, demoralized, and likely to collapse entirely if confronted with a large airborne attack."
>
> "Market-Garden" went ahead—but not quite as planned. Instead of encountering a few old men who collapsed or ran away, 1st Airborne Division fell upon a hornets' nest of German armour. Far from being demoralized, the enemy fought like tigers to defend the gateway to their homeland.[4]

Decisions are streams of choices. While each choice might be treated as a discrete event and each subproblem might be considered a discrete problem, the choices accumulate either by design or happen-stance. At some point, the accumulation builds a momentum of its own that can sweep up even well-intentioned decision makers.

Subsequent investigation showed without doubt that the design of the O-ring seals on the space shuttle Challenger was inadequate to prevent the leakage of fuel that, on January 28, 1986, caused a fatal explosion shortly after launch. The investigation, documented by the President's Commission report, also revealed that the inadequacy of the engineering design was known within the contracting company and that the potential danger had been documented by internal memos.[5] Nonetheless, when the launch decision had to be made, "Thiokol management reversed its position and recommended the launch of [the Challenger] at the urging of [NASA] and contrary to the views of its engineers in order to accommodate a major customer."[6]

While Thiokol maintains that it never agreed to launch in weather as cold as it was, there is no question that serious breakdowns occurred within the hierarchies of both Thiokol and NASA. No one intended to cause a catastrophe that killed seven people, virtually derailed the space program for two years, and seriously dented the credibility of NASA. Nor did the people involved deliberately invite the question later asked by some NASA employees' children: "Mommy, Daddy, were you responsible for killing the astronauts?"[7] No, the explanation lies much deeper and involves well-meaning managers caught up in events, victims of systems they created or simply found themselves in.

If decisions can be viewed as streams—streams containing countless bits of information, events, and choices—then how should decision makers be viewed? In organized settings the people charged with making the decisions are located in formal leadership roles as managers, administrators, officers, or whatever. The streams flowing through the organization do not wait for them; they flow around them. The streams do not serve up problems neatly wrapped and ready for choice. Rather, they deliver the bits and pieces, the problems and choices, in no particular order. For the individual manager, daily life is a montage of things to be done.

> ... management, in large measure, is dealing with the unexpected that interferes with expectations and routines, with unanticipated crises and petty little problems that require much more time than they're worth.
> ... The manager may well go from a budget meeting involving millions to a discussion of what to do about a broken decorative water fountain.[8]

In short, decision makers in an organization are floating in the stream, jostled capriciously by problems popping up, and finding anchors through action at a given time in a given place. The importance of the problem to the organization often is not the determining factor in the time and effort consumed. It may be unclear just how important a prob-

THE ACCUMULATION
OF CHOICES BUILDS A
MOMENTUM OF ITS OWN.

lem is, or there may be many different ways to define a clearly important problem. Was the balky cargo latch a nuisance or the most important item in a long list of other defects? Was deciding to use the A-bomb more or less important than the many other agenda items at Potsdam, for instance determining the boundaries of occupied Germany or the governance of Poland? Was information on troop concentrations around Arnhem more or less believable or significant than countless other intelligence reports (including, incidentally, the discovery of plywood tanks used by the Germans to mislead Allied reconnaissance)? Was the potential hazard of the O-rings at low temperature a truly life-threatening danger or an overly conservative reaction from a space program that had lost its daring? What in retrospect is crystal clear to everyone else is often problematic to the individuals involved at the time.

Fortunately, life in organizations doesn't require managers to make such grim decisions every day. Instead of A-bombs and shuttle launches, the daily fare more likely requires dealing with a balky contractor, a resource shortage, reorganization, or any of a number of problems arising from the day-to-day operations of an organization. But is there any reason to believe that the processes associated with more mundane decisions will be more orderly, more carefully considered, than those involved in high magnitude problems? In the day-to-day business of organizational life, decision making is seldom the logical, rational, systematic process suggested by the management textbooks.[9] It does not unfold in identifiable stages where a problem is defined, alternative solutions are generated, the alternatives are weighed against a known criterion, and a choice is made.[10] The stages are instead inextricably intertwined; discovering what exactly the problem is all about is conjoined with the identification of alternatives and their evaluation. Often a choice is made quite early in the process, with subsequent activity devoted to confirming the early choice. (This is true, for example, even in the processes of jury deliberation.[11])

The stages of the decision-making process are intertwined because managers constantly alternate between knowledge generation and action. In day-to-day practice, managers show an appreciation for "the intimate connection between thought and action".[12] Based on research about how senior managers think, Isenberg found that in managerial action "thinking is inseparable from acting"; managing is a "dynamic, interactive series of activity and reflection."[13] Schon argued that managers, among other professionals, are reflective practitioners who "reflect-in-action [which] consists in on-the-spot surfacing, criticizing, restructuring, and testing of intuitive understandings."[14] He called for a management science that appreciates the artistry by which managers build models as a basis for action and use action to conduct knowledge-bearing experiments. Torbert contributed to such a management science by developing the notion of "action-inquiry," which is a method by which skillful managers weave together knowledge generation and action by constantly questioning and, if necessary, revising the assumptions that support action.[15]

We begin, then, by looking at how information, events, and situations come to be recognized as problems in the first place. It is important to note that recognition and definition of problems are not necessarily the same. To recognize a problem means to be aware that "something is wrong." Generally, this includes at least a vague awareness of what that "something" is, but the definition of a problem is likely to evolve throughout the decision-making process.

# 2

# *MANAGERIAL PROBLEMS: THE EMERGENCE OF MEANING*

Most of the research on decision making starts with a recognized and defined problem: The task of the decision maker is to come up with a solution. As we reviewed the research, we could find very little on the nature of the problems faced by managers, where the problems came from, or how they got defined. What little we could find about "problem finding,"[1] as well as what is known about the complexity of managerial jobs,[2] suggested that figuring out what the problem is might be half the battle, especially in a managerial environment.

To explore this issue, we began by asking managers two simple questions: "What kinds of problems do you deal with every day?" and "To what extent are these problems clearly defined when they get to you?"

## WHAT ARE THE PROBLEMS?

I think at one time or another I've been involved with every kind of problem there is. I don't know of any I've been lucky enough to escape. (Company president)

PROBLEM...SOMETHING THROWN FORWARD.

The things that managers have to decide about are, as one might expect, highly diverse. They range from gut-wrenching personnel decisions ("I guess the hardest decisions really involve letting some good people go—people in key positions that you've worked with for years who may have developed mental problems, or family problems, or liquor problems that they couldn't overcome") to decisions involving huge financial risks ("This was a multimillion dollar venture and we didn't have any time to lay the groundwork if we were to get into the game"). They involve the mundane (assigning parking spaces, remodeling the cafeteria) and the colossal (opening the doors for trade with China, setting up joint ventures overseas). And they involve the myriad of issues that affect "getting the product out the door" while remaining solvent:

> [The problem] could be in a competitive area where prices are being cut. It could be not having the kind of equipment to do a certain type of work. It could be not having the right people to do the job. It could be not having the right kind of financing.

No matter whom we talked to—whether first-level manager or company president, whether the company was large or small—the diversity of problems was astonishing. Asked for examples of immediate issues facing them, eleven general managers responded with items like the following:

- getting rid of 75 rail cars that everyone dealing with a shutdown forgot about—creating a cash drain of $2.5 million;
- a problem with a competitor who is also a supplier;
- news of an infringement on a patent for a major product;
- a phone call from a customer wanting to buy one of the division's small businesses;
- a phone call from a supplier who wants to sell a piece of equity in his business;
- a proposal the GM made to headquarters to install a system of incentive compensation in the division—the corporation is resisting;
- a $2 million claim against the company made by a customer in France—"We screwed them and now we have to negotiate";
- a meeting with a supplier about a new product it has come up with;
- a meeting to troubleshoot problems with a pilot plant for a new product;
- a bid from a major customer (to buy large quantities of the company's product);
- a decision on a price increase and how to increase the chances of its being accepted;
- how to get approval from a federal regulatory agency for a new kind of product;
- how to export a new product that is still prohibited in the U.S.;
- a meeting with U.K. representatives on incentives they will offer the company to build a plant there;
- a personnel change in a key position;
- a customer's request for a price concession on a product that lost $16 million last year.[3]

These and many other items of lesser and greater significance constitute the daily fare of general managers. As our GM told us, "Every hour is filled with these kinds of issues."

Although most of the general managers' issues listed above are business related, managers spend a great deal of their time dealing with *process* problems: how to organize to solve business problems. In a study of how executives think, Isenberg determined that "foremost among their conscious thoughts are the processes for accomplishing a change or implementing a decision."[4] Whose support do they need and how can it be obtained? Whose likely resistance must be overcome and how? What mechanisms need to be put into place to achieve the desired outcome?

We also found that managers seldom face just one problem at a time.

At one point we asked forty managers to list the problems they had on their desks and found that on a given day managers had an average of five issues to confront, not counting the unexpected crises that were likely to appear. Further, the problems that confront managers at a given time are often interrelated so that action on one must be taken in light of the problem's relation to others.[5] A general manager knows that if he decides to raise prices as a way of increasing profits, he may open the door to increased competition which could eventually cut into market share and lower profits.

Another feature was the problems most often appeared with little regard for the manager's schedule.

> You just have to make time in the schedule to do the things that are important when they come. If it's a ten-hour day, well that's fine. Or if it's twelve or fourteen you still have to go ahead and do it. Period.

Because there are new problems each day, and because many problems get worse if they are ignored, managers talked continually about "identifying problems early" and "nipping them in the bud." As we shall see later, this ability to detect problems early not only helps in day-to-day decision making but can be essential in handling crises (see Chapter 4). An especially tricky aspect of managerial decision making is that managers themselves may be implicated in any problem they pick up. Maybe that turnover problem is somehow related to the manager's leadership style; perhaps the cautious, slow-to-innovate posture of the organization derives from the manager's autocratic, risk-averse approach to leading. As much as managers may want to treat problems as residing entirely outside themselves, they must be continually open to understanding *themselves* in relation to problems.[6]

The portrait of managerial problems that emerged was a blending of complexity, diversity, fast pace, and lack of control over when problems appeared. In this context, the derivation of the word *problem* is interesting. It is derived from the Greek word *proballein* which is the composite of *pro,* meaning forward, and *ballein,* meaning to throw. Thus, *problem* literally means "something thrown forward."

## ARE THE PROBLEMS CLEARLY DEFINED?

As one might expect in the maelstrom of things thrown forward, some problems are well defined from the outset, either in fact or at first glance. As one company president put it:

> In a small corporation there is never any problem knowing what the problem is. There's likely to be some guy in there pounding at your door threatening to whip you.

In some cases, not only is the problem well defined, but it is presented to the manager with a solution already attached. "The engineering drawings are late; we need more people to get them out on time."

In the corporate setting, the balance is a primary herald of problems:

> You find out about your problems when you look at financial statements. If you're not operating at a profit, you have a problem of varying degrees. When you start running into red ink, the problem gets progressively more serious as the months progress and you run into more red ink.

In fact, much of a manager's job involves the identification of discrepancies—differences between an existing and a desired state of affairs—that announce the presence of problems.[7]

Managers sometimes detect discrepancies by comparing an existing state of affairs against some standard. One such standard is the past, against which managers continually compare the present in search of differences. Quantitative indicators lend themselves well to this kind of monitoring:

> Why is our inventory drifting out of line? Why is our reject rate so high this week? What has happened to make so many deliveries late? What can be done to reverse the trend in absenteeism? Why is our safety record suddenly

so good? All these problems and a host of others can keep a manager and his organization busy all day every day.[8]

A second yardstick used in organizations is plans and forecasts. Managers are evaluated against the goals to which they committed themselves.[9] They are held responsible for reaching certain levels of sales, profits, costs, and other performance variables.[10] Above these levels the rule is, "If it ain't broke, don't fix it." But if a variable falls below the planned-for level, a manager faces a problematic situation calling for some kind of resolution. A third standard applied to the performance of a manager's unit is the performance of other, presumably comparable, units within the same organization and sometimes in other organizations.

Discrepancies of these three kinds indicate the possible existence of a problem. The first sign of trouble sometimes tells the whole story, but not very often. When word of a problem first reaches a manager, it signals the beginning of the attempt to "find" the problem. As the problem begins to appear, its recognition triggers a series of search-and-interpret missions to reveal what lies beneath the surface. So even when their presence is clearly signaled, the true scope and meaning of problems can remain submerged.

In the extreme case of an ill-defined problem, its very presence must be intuited (and could easily be missed) and its meaning is deeply buried:

> Every problem you have is because there is something wrong with the design—of the system, or the product, or the management, or the selection process—otherwise you wouldn't have a problem.
>
> You have to be really good at clues because you get clues from people or you see things happen that just don't seem to fit together. If you don't try to figure out why, you think it's just one of those things that "just happened to happen." (Corporate vice-president)

Such problems evoke an image of the manager as sleuth, a far cry from the pugilistic manager facing "some guy at the door threatening to whip you."

There is clearly, then, a continuum of problems that lands on a manager's desk, from the virtually prepackaged to the completely ill-defined. To get some idea of how problems are distributed along this continuum, we again asked our forty managers to consider the problems they had on their desks. We asked them to arrange their problems along a five-point scale, with "1" indicating the prepackaged and "5" the ill-defined. The result was almost even distribution of the 214 problems, with approximately equal numbers at each point on the continuum:

| PREPACKAGED | | | | ILL-DEFINED |
|---|---|---|---|---|
| 1 | 2 | 3 | 4 | 5 |
| 22.4% | 18.2% | 22.9% | 15.4% | 21.1% |

PROBLEMS RARELY COME GIFT-WRAPPED.
OF COURSE, THERE ARE OCCASIONAL EXCEPTIONS.

What is "thrown forward" may be crisp and clear, or it may be an enigmatic clue to some amorphous beast lurking out there. But even in the clearest case—the clear problem that comes complete with solution—what meets the eye may have little to do with reality. Earlier we mentioned that the engineering drawings were late, and more people were needed to get them done on time. Add one fact: The product was still getting out on time in spite of the late drawings. One might conclude now that the due dates were wrong—that the drawings weren't needed any earlier and therefore the staff was adequate. Or, as the manager in this case finally discovered, that the drawings weren't needed at all, and the unit was in fact overstaffed.

What all this means is that the problems managers face are, in reality, clusters of information and observations from which meaning emerges. There is more than a grain of truth in the aphorism that "a problem is what you make of it." What is thrown in the manager's direction may be raw information, analysis, or explicit statements of problems. Those who are throwing the problems may thrown them straight or toss curves. On its way to the manager, the problem may fly unimpeded, or it may be transformed in some way, or even be intercepted.

In these metaphorical terms, we mean to suggest the unpredictability of recognizing problems in organizations. Stressing the failures in the intelligence-gathering process, Wilensky described the vagaries of recognition:

> Sources of failure are legion: even if the initial message is accurate, clear, timely, and relevant, it may be translated, condensed, or completely blocked

by personnel standing between the sender and the intended receiver; it may get through in distorted form. If the receiver is in a position to use the message, he may screen it out because it does not fit his preconceptions, because it has come through a suspicious or poorly regarded channel, because it is embedded in piles of inaccurate or useless messages (excessive noise in the channel), or, simply, because too many messages are transmitted to him (information overload).[11]

Streams of information, events, old problems, and previous decisions flow directly, or through a maze of intermediate channels, to a manager who, in turn, fashions meaning from them. To understand how problems get defined, we must understand two things about information: first, how it gets sorted, filtered, and organized; and second, how the individual manager, alone or in concert with others, fashions meaning from it. While these two elements are not always separate, we'll examine them sepa-

STREAMS OF INFORMATION FROM MANY
CHANNELS CONVERGE ON THE MANAGER.

rately. First, we will look at the flow of information; then we will see how managers make sense of information.

## THE FLOW OF INFORMATION

Managers can be called "information workers"; a manager is a craftsperson whose raw material is information. Most managers spend most of their time with other people, and with these people they go about the business of exchanging information.[12] What little time managers get to themselves, uninterrupted by people or calls, they spend reading (absorbing information), thinking (processing information), and writing (disseminating information). Theirs is a craft in which meaning and decisions are fashioned from the whole cloth of information.

But an information worker is only as good as the material he or she has to work with. Thus, we come to the question: Where does a manager's information come from? Managers have many sources, including (a) systems and structures set up to keep them apprised of ongoing events, (b) the people around them who volunteer information and can be approached in search of trouble signs, clues, and missing pieces of puzzles, (c) the values of the organization, which point people in certain directions and define the critical variables in a complex array of possibilities, and (d) the manager's own direct experience.

### Systems, Structures, and the Flow of Information

Important aids to a manager's continuing quest to stay on top of developments in his or her area of responsibility are the various formal management information systems. These systems process data on innumerable aspects of organizational performance. These data are condensed into indicators by which departures from past performance or deviation against future targets can be detected readily: Their importance to managers cannot be underestimated. Like the control panel in the DC-10, these indicators are the warning lights and buzzers that monitor vital systems.

While information systems serve managers, they also play to human weaknesses. For example, people (and managers in particular) are inveterate seekers of information, and given some uncertainty, they will seek more information than is required. As numerous studies have shown,[13] beyond a certain point, more information does *not* improve the accuracy of decisions, but it does increase the decision maker's confidence in, and satisfaction with, the decision. By making available almost limitless data, a complex information system can contribute to managerial information overload and result in a paralysis of action.[14] Further, access to large amounts of information has been shown to result in *selective use* of that information to bolster a preconceived position, leading some managers to focus on the information supporting their decision while ignoring the information that goes against it.[15]

Because of their quantitative and logical formats, information systems can have additional detrimental effects. For example, Hogarth and Makridakis reviewed studies showing that "logical data displays" can cause people to overlook critical pieces of a problem that are not addressed in the underlying logic of the data analysis. The internally consistent logic may belie the fact that the basic assumptions were faulty or incomplete, or that the data comprising them were questionable in the first place ("garbage in, garbage out").

Also, the availability of quantitative analysis, particularly in efforts to forecast the future, can lead to a dependency on such analysis; this may increase managerial comfort without improving accuracy. This situation can be so pronounced that managers lose sight of the costs of additional information:

> A recent case that came to our attention was the expenditure of $20 million to plan and forecast a $160 million investment. However, a detailed analysis of the situation and possible errors in forecasts indicated that even perfectly accurate forecasts would not be worth anything like $20 million. In some situations, even perfect knowledge of the future has relatively little value.[16]

Even under the best of circumstances, formal information systems simply point out that a problem may exist. The meaning of a discrepancy in the numbers, and often whether or not a discrepancy is significant, remains a managerial judgment.

Information systems are one way that information gets to the manager. Additional formal channels for transmitting information to the right people are provided by organizational structure. "A basic function of an organization structure is to channel problems which are identified by its various members to individuals especially qualified to solve them.[17]

Hierarchy is one fundamental organizational arrangement that serves this function: Certain people are given responsibility for the novel or unexpected events occurring in the areas below them.[18] But, even for managers with impressive mental capabilities, information flowing through the hierarchy can become overabundant. Kotter describes the plight of the general manager:

> In the case of a typical GM, thousands of people, most of whom were not physically located close to him, were somehow involved in his operations on a daily basis. Under these circumstances, simply trying to monitor daily or weekly operational activity can be extremely difficult. The most impressive

information-systems technology available today cannot monitor all this activity quickly and accurately. Even if it could, a GM could spend twenty-four hours a day simply trying to digest that information. Furthermore, under these circumstances, the sheer volume of relatively minor short-run problems can be enormous.[19]

This kind of assault upon a manager's senses can lead to information overload. Let us say that a manager is responsible for a plant in which various structures, policies, and procedures are available to govern the routine operation of the plant. When exceptions on the shop floor arise, they are frequently referred to the manager. "That is, the new situation, for which there is no preplanned response, is referred upward in the hierarchy to permit the creation of a new response."[20] The result is that as more new situations occur, and as more exceptions are referred upwards, the manager eventually becomes overwhelmed.

Specialization is another basic type of organizational structure that channels problems and information by setting up functional units responsible for certain classes of problems. This division of labor is necessary because many complex problems exceed the capacity of one or a few individuals to comprehend. As a result, problems are broken down into manageable pieces and assigned to different functional units. Specialization aids problem recognition by limiting the sights of each set of specialists, thus making it easier for them to recognize the problems of special relevance to them. Specialization also helps by giving the organization a clearly designated place to route certain classes of problems.

Unfortunately, specialization, like hierarchy, enables but also impedes problem recognition. Specialization is notorious for leading to rivalries among specialists and a corresponding tendency to distort information to advance the interests of a speciality. Wilensky gave an example related to Pearl Harbor:

> In the armed forces, intense rivalries between services and within service—among supply and procurement, plans and operations, research and development, intelligence—lead to intelligence failures. . . . In 1941, the signals of the pending attack on Pearl Harbor lay scattered in a number of rival agencies; communication lines linked them but essential messages never flowed across the lines, let alone to the top. The Army and Navy presented a picture of cordial, respectful communication, empty of solid substance.[21]

A further difficulty associated with specialization is that information sometimes ends up in the wrong function. Preoccupied with their own specialized area and lacking a firm grasp of other specialties, functional managers may not transmit the information to the right place. The more ambiguous or novel the information, the more likely it is that channeling mistakes will be made.

In summary, tried-and-true structures like hierarchy and specialization, and the new information technologies, serve major roles in the recognition and definition of managerial problems. With the aid of these methods, bits and pieces of information are sorted, sifted, analyzed, and channeled in more or less usable form to more or less the right people. Systems and structure, however, are seriously limited in many ways. Most managers recognize this, realizing that ultimately other *people* are the major source of information.

## Other People as Sources of Informaiton

Managers are dependent on the people around them to provide needed information. As one executive put it: "What else is there to do but talk to the people who work for you, and your customers, and your suppliers?" But even under the best conditions, people volunteer information to the manager only up to a point, and then powerful inhibitors take over.

People who bring information to a manager are sensitive to the reception they get, and nothing shuts them off faster than a discouraging response. Some managers treat others who conscientiously call a problem to their attention as if *they* were the problem. It takes only one or two "beheadings" to stop people from bringing bad news, especially subordinates. In some cases, even a lack of interest is sufficient to inhibit the flow of information. An agency director we know did not seem to care about the performance of the units reporting to her, and, as a result, her department heads were only too willing to smooth over shortfalls in the performance of their programs.

The problem of getting reliable information from others is especially pronounced when those others are subordinates. Managers have the power to reward and punish, giving subordinates an incentive to find and dispose of problems. But dependence also creates a disincentive to report information that may cause a loss of favor. In one study of fifty-two managers and their direct superiors, it was found that managers were more likely to withhold information about problems in their work if either of two conditions existed: The managers had strong ambitions for advancement, or they didn't trust their superiors.[22] Similarly, Lyles and Mitroff, in a study of thirty-three upper-level managers, found that:

> Fear and political power were recurring themes affecting the formulation of problems. At all organizational levels there were individuals with fears caused by various pressures such as personal failure, threats of punishment, organization failure, or time constraints. Fear of punishment or failure could even cause a person to try to cover up the real problem.... Some managers obscured problems and even deliberately distorted information in order to protect their positions. Thus, any formulation of a problem that identified conflict or past errors in judgment was avoided or obscured.[23]

As Wilensky put it, "In reporting at every level, hierarchy is conducive to concealment and misrepresentation; subordinates are asked to transmit information that can be used to evaluate their performance."[24] Thus, powerful dynamics can cut off decision makers from their supply of information, and problems and negative information are not necessarily "thrown forward" to them.

Given the inhibitors to a full flow of information, managers cannot affort to wait for information to come to them. Not only must they actively encourage people to keep them informed, they must actively pursue information themselves. In an in-depth study of fifteen general managers, Kotter found that what distinguished effective from less effective managers was how aggressively they sought information.[25] Bennis has noted that "people in power have to work very hard at getting people to tell them the truth; the right people will, and the right bosses will hear it.[26] Halberstam provides an object lesson on this point in an anecdote about a briefing that Robert Kennedy, as attorney general, received in 1962 on a trip to Saigon:

> He was supposed to be briefed at the airport terminal by [top staff members] all of whom, in one another's presence, assured him that everything was on target. "Do you have any problems?" he asked. No, said everyone in unison, there were no problems. He looked at them somewhat shocked by the response. "No problems," he said, "you've really got no problems? Does anyone here want to speak to me in private about his problems?" And then one by one they talked to him at length and it all came pouring out. . . .[27]

Managers keep their fingers on the pulse by cultivating a network of job-relevant relationships and by staying in regular contact with the people in their network. A manager may well be in *daily* contact with key people.[28]

Another aggressive strategy for rooting out information is going outside normal channels. If formal channels block or distort information flow, the executive does well to "cut new channels of intelligence," especially for novel or extraordinary problems. They "bypass the regular machinery and seek firsthand exposure to intelligence sources in and out of the organization."[29] Sayles and Chandler have described this an an improvised give-and-take geared toward identifying and eventually solving specific problems.[30]

Thus, organizational machinery such as formal information systems, and formal channels of communication keep the manager informed—up to a point. But effective managers take an aggressive posture toward getting information from other people. They ferret out what is useful from the pile of information arriving on its own and root out further information that would otherwise never make it because of the powerful constraints that sometimes prevent information from flowing in organizations.

## Values as Information Conduits

No discussion of the sources of information in an organizational setting is complete without considering organizational "culture" or "values." While systems, structures, and people are tangible (if erratic) sources of information, values are often quite nebulous (though a strong enough value system may translate into quantifiable standards). The impetus for this discussion comes from a book that attempts to identify the sources of excellence in effective companies:

> Virtually all of the better performing companies we looked at ... had a well-defined set of guiding beliefs. The less well-performing institutions, on the other hand, were marked by one of two characteristics. Many had no set of coherent beliefs. The other had distinctive and widely discussed objectives.[31]

Throughout their book, Peters and Waterman give examples of corporate values that have profound effects on the types of information to which managers attend. Unlike specific objectives or other situationally induced reactions, these values are etched into the corporate fabric. For example, IBM's emphasis on service to the customer is described by the authors as an obsession. This emphasis probably leads IBM managers to search for customer-related information in a totally different way than do managers in a company without such values. Frito Lay provides another example with its "99.5 percent service level" (all customers stand a 99.5 percent chance of getting a daily call from a route salesperson), a goal that can't help but sensitize managers in Frito Lay to information that would not be seen as important somewhere else.

Another example, in a different sphere, also comes from IBM. Peters and Waterman quote an IBM executive as saying:

> You can foul up on most anything and you'll get another chance. But if you screw up, even a little bit, on people management, you're gone. That's it, top performer or not.[32]

While this may be an overstatement, even a semblance of value that strong has to result in a greater sensitivity to information about the people who work for you.

By referring to corporate values as sources of information about problems, we are not ignoring the importance of the values individuals bring to the system. Rather, we are suggesting that overriding corporate themes affect large numbers of managers in similar ways and can result in quite different information patterns in different companies. These larger values can have pervasive effects on

- what information is considered relevant
- what data are collected systematically
- who sees the data
- who cares about it.

The result, we would guess, is that managers "see" more customer service problems in IBM and Frito Lay than elsewhere, not because there are more problems, but because they are more focused on such information. Information relevant to the value theme is more likely to reach the manager, in more detail, and have more implications. Thus, the threshold at which information reveals a problem is lower.

### Direct Experience

A final source of the bits and pieces that become problems—and perhaps the most compelling source—is the direct, hands-on experience of a manager. There is research evidence that concrete information based on firsthand experience dominates secondhand information,[33] or as General Patton observed, "one look is worth a hundred reports."[34] The theme of "seeing for yourself" pervades our interviews with managers and executives, and it covers virtually all aspects of the business. They repeatedly describe how, as a result of their own direct effort, they got to know about things such as the following:

The boss:

You've got to understand where his hot buttons are.

Information sources:

When you know your organization pretty well, you have a pretty good idea who's giving you the straight dope and who's trying to beat around the bush.

Company directors:

You generally know who's on your side on the board of directors and you might approach those individuals . . . to discuss it with them before you present it to the whole board.

The city:

I've lived around here a long time. I know a lot of people. I make it my business to study things as well as I can: area and locations, the way the city is growing. It's part of my job to locate our operations in the best possible sites.

The business:

The first thing I did was get out on those raggedy old [oil] rigs and get to know the people in the organization and the customers—I got to know as many of them as quickly as I could.

Employees:

You have to have some people around you that can help you when you need help. You have to have someone who is competent in operations, in your comptroller's end of the thing, in sales. When it comes right down to it, they're the people you have to call on to do the job.

This theme—you've got to know it firsthand—underlies all phases of the decision-making process.[35] To recognize a problem you've "got to have a feel for it"; to establish the credibility of your sources you've "got to know the people"; to trust the numbers you've "got to know where they came from." It is this intimate knowledge, this personal understanding of the business and the people associated with it that allows managers to sift through the overload of information, to pick out the bits and pieces that singly or together define important problems:

You have to know. You have to have very keen hearing. It comes at you in very unique ways, ways you never expect it. You hear one thing here, one thing there, and you've got to put that story together in your mind. Now a lot of times the thing you fabricate is wrong, but by the very act of trying to put it together, you get more data.

## The Flotsam and Jetsam That Become Problems—A Summary

There is no shortage of raw information from which problems are fashioned. Organizational systems and structures, constant interaction with a wide variety of people, strong corporate beliefs and values, and direct experience all channel, sort, organize, and otherwise influence the information flowing to a manager. Sometimes the meaning of the bits and pieces is immediately evident; getting the information and recognizing the problem are simultaneous. More often, however, the manager must dig, must struggle with the linkages, to fashion meaning. Because of the ambiguity in the raw information, the fallibility of the systems, structures, and people that channel and interpret it, and the inherent limits of individuals as they process complex information, problem finding is—well, problematic.

As we stated early in the book, decision making does not unfold in discrete, sequential stages. We are already forcing a distinction between the information available to a manager (the previous section) and making sense of that information (the topic of the following section). Getting information and knowing what the problem is often occur simultaneously, and sometimes solutions emerge along with them. But we believe that for a high percentage of problems, meaning does not spring forth, but rather emerges slowly. Meaning can emerge as the manager digs for information (or stumbles into it) and gradually sees connections that define a problem. It can emerge as successive definitions of the problem are refined, modified, or discarded with the advent of more information. Or, it may emerge from a more complex and somewhat disorderly process of trial and error, where information, interpretation, and action intermingle, at some point revealing the "real" problem.

## MAKING SENSE OF THE PIECES

Because of the complexity already noted, information, events, and observations are not themselves "problems"—there is instead some process by which meaning is attached to raw information. It may be instantaneous— as an experienced pilot's response to a warning light—or it may be more labored—as when a committee struggles for months to get all the facts together and draw a conclusion. The more novel, ambiguous, or complex the problem is, the more difficult it will be to put the informational pieces together, and the more likely it is that early problem statements will be erroneous or simplistic.

This section, then, addresses the issue of interpolation—making sense of the pieces. Once information reaches a manager, by whatever route, how is it used to recognize problems? As managers confront incoming information, they are first of all affected by the fact that all human beings can only process so much information, and fallibly at that. Second, as they attempt to interpret the data, they are aided (and hindered) by their own experience—all people simplify the world by constructing mental "maps" of what causes what, what is connected to what. We must simplify to survive. Third, neither managers nor scientists, no matter how valiantly they strive for objectivity, are emotionally neutral about the problems they face. And fourth, managers define reality not only in their own heads but in conjunction with the people around them. Because people often disagree about what reality is, "my reality or yours" may have to be decided by negotiation.

### You Can Only Process So Much

Because information is the lifeblood of a manager's job, the good manager welcomes it, encourages it, and goes after it. As we have clearly suggested, without an ample and regular supply of valid information, a

MANAGERS HAVE TO SHAPE REALITY.

manager wouldn't know about emergent problems, much less be able to do anything about them. But human information-processing capability is limited, and managers are not exempt. It has been estimated, for example, that managers can retain only 1/100 to 1/1000 of the information to which they are exposed.[36] Furthermore, most people are able to hold in short-term memory only about seven pieces of information.[37] Albeit impressive, human cognitive ability is indisputably bounded.[38]

Managers cope with the profusion of stimuli by employing strategies that make the task more manageable. To stretch short-term memory, for example, people "chunk" events together so as to retain greater amounts of information. If the approximately seven bits of information consist of small *patterns,* themselves containing bits of information, then the ability to retain and process information is increased several fold.[39] Another strategy is to "segment" the stream of stimuli into smaller, familiar units that can be worked on sequentially.[40] Thus, managers don't deal with raw information bit by bit, but interpret it in terms of *preexisting* categories or patterns. This creates a tendency to force incoming information into pre-existing mind sets, even if it doesn't really fit.

Of all the areas of research on decision making, the biases (limits) associated with processing information are by far the best documented. Managers, perhaps more than the rest of us, confront a complex environment characterized by information overload and pressure to act on incomplete (and often ambiguous) data. And the pitfalls are legion. To give you

TABLE 2-1    A Few of the Many Information Processing Biases

| Bias/Source of Bias | Description/Example |
|---|---|
| Availability | • If a person can easily recall specific instances of an event, he/she may overestimate how frequently the event occurs (and vice versa).<br>• Chance events or cues can hinder or help by pointing a person in a particular direction. |
| Selective Perception | • What one expects to see biases what one does see.<br>• People seek information consistent with their own views.<br>• People downplay information that conflicts with a consistent profile. |
| Concrete Information | • Vivid, direct experience dominates abstract information; a single personal experience can outweigh more valid statistical information. |
| Data Presentation | • The items presented first (primacy) or last (recency) in a series assume undue importance.<br>• Whether information is collected sequentially or all at once affects what is processed. |
| Inconsistency | • People have trouble applying a consistent judgmental strategy across similar cases, even though they believe they are consistent. |
| Law of Small Numbers | • Small samples are deemed representative of the larger population (a few cases "prove the rule"), even when they are not. |
| Complexity | • Under time pressure, processing of complex information may be quite superficial. |
| Gambler's Fallacy | • Seeing an unexpected number of similar chance events leads to belief that an event not seen will occur (e.g., after observing 9 successive reds in roulette, believing chances for a black on the next roll are greater than 50/50). |

Condensed and adapted from Robin M. Hogarth and Spyros Makridakis, Forecasting and Planning: An Evaluation, *Management Science,* Vol. 27, No. 2., February 1981, pp. 117–120.

an idea of just how awesome human bias is, we've adapted a summary table (Table 2-1) from a recent review of research by Hogarth and Makridakis.[41]

## We Have to Simplify to Survive

But we're not finished yet. Information, already distorted, still must be aggregated into a coherent view of "a problem." One way that people cope with an abundance of information—with the "bloomin', buzzin' confusion"—is to slice it up into their own cognitive categories. Individuals depend on their intricate web of "personal constructs" to channel their perceptions and actions,[42] and managers similarly employ maps of their world to help them see what is relevant to their work. This cognitive set is indispensable to managers threatened by a high tide of information. Managers develop mental sets according to their function, history, level, and prospects in an organization.

Function plays an important part. In one study, sales managers and production managers were exposed to the same information, but what registered for each set of managers was the information related to the goals and activities of their own function.[43] More recently, Gabarro studied new general managers as they "took charge" and found that for thirteen of fourteen "their initial actions were in areas where they had functional experience, and the most significant changes they made during the three years also were in the areas where they had experience."[44] Managers who have worked in several different functions are less likely to identify exclusively with their current functions than managers who have been brought up in a single function.[45] Level in the organization is also crucial. The outlook and concerns of top-level executives differ markedly from those of middle managers, which in turn depart significantly from those of first-line supervisors. A study found that attitudes toward the company became more positive when workers were promoted to foremen, but attitudes returned to their original state when an economic downturn caused the foremen to be demoted back to workers.[46] In general, managers' prospects for advancement influence their view of the organization: Upwardly mobile individuals approach their jobs and their relationships quite differently from the less mobile and the "stuck."[47]

Unfortunately, as with organizational structure, cognitive structure helps but also hinders. The drawback of a mental set is that, just as it helps a manager tune in needed elements in the stream of input, it may lead a manager to tune out potentially important information. Managers work hard to resolve ambiguity by getting a fix on a situation, and they can be most reluctant to surrender the fix once they have it. Frequently, "when confronted with a fact inconsistent with a fixed idea, the perceiver distorts the data to eliminate the inconsistency."[48] Preconceptions resist new conceptions. Recall the example from Chapter 1 in which Allied commanders, preparing to attack the Arnhem area of Holland, gave short shrift to accurate reports of German units in the area. Another dramatic example from World War II was the failure to prepare for the distinct possibility of a Japanese attack on Pearl Harbor. Admiral Kimmel, commander in chief of the Pacific Fleet, stuck to his original plan for mobilizing for the war in the Pacific, despite the immediate threat of attack:

> Admiral Kimmel and his staff continued to cling to the policy to which they had committed themselves, discounting each fresh warning and failing to note that more and more signs were pointing to the possibility that Pearl Harbor might be a target for a surprise attack. They repeatedly renewed their decision to continue using the available resources primarily for training green sailors and soldiers and for supplying bases close to Japan, rather than instituting an adequate alert that would give priority to defending Pearl Harbor against enemy attack.[49]

Managers sometimes can't see what they believe can't be there; as one said, "there is difficulty convincing people there is a problem when people don't believe the problem could exist."[50]

One's images of the world resist change, especially when those images have stood up over time.[51] If an agency has always enjoyed adequate federal funding, then it may not take seriously the early signs of a deteriorating situation. If a company has always "taken care of its people," it will be hard to believe reports that layoffs are imminent. When circumstances change gradually, the original image may persist even though the reality slips further away.[52] Because of this durability, it sometimes takes a powerful stimulus like a crisis or even a catastrophe to break a mental set. Complaints from customers about quality problems may not be taken seriously, for example, until a major customer decides to go elsewhere.

Managers also resist changing their mental sets when change seems painful or difficult. Like the rest of us, they would almost prefer not to know about something they feel they can do nothing about.

Thus, cognitive maps serve a useful purpose in problem recognition, but they also pose a hazard when they are not revised or replaced in light of fresh experience. The challenge is for managers to "detect the subtle discontinuities that may undermine a business in the future."[53]

### The Emotional Component

As managers think about information and talk things through with others, they become to some degree emotionally involved with the problems discovered. For one thing, to acknowledge a problem usually means adding one more item to an already considerable workload; new problems mean added pressures. For another thing, a discrepancy can be threatening. When a negative signal appears in a manager's bailiwick, it can be a commentary on that manager's performance. Thus, managers are not cool and detached observers of their organizational scenes. They are invested in their points of view, policies, and ways of doing things, and they are identified with the fate of their people and their organizations. To comtemplate a problem is not a cool mental act but "hot cognition."[54] Every time a new problem appears on the horizon, a manager experiences something ranging from a twinge to a shock, from mild interest to considerable excitement. The problem is both a threat to the existing order and an opportunity to restore or enhance that order. Thus, managers are *involved,* directly or indirectly, in what they observe: They are as much participants as observers. Commenting on his novel, *The Golden Bowl,* Henry James said about the characters as observers of the events around them: "There is no other participant [in the novel], of course, than each of the real, the deeply involved and immersed and more or less bleeding participants."[55] While managers tend to pride themselves on emotional detachment, the stories they told us were hardly sterile:

> You have a budget set up on a project to get it done within a certain time and for a certain price. The figures come to you, indicating you're going to get it done on that basis. Then, at the last minute, you find out you're going to have a big overrun. All of a sudden you have to face up to the thing and go to the board of directors and whoever else is involved to tell them you goofed and what it's going to take to bail you out of it. It's a *real embarrassing thing to do.* You can't lay the blame on your organization because, any way you look at it, you're responsible.

And another:

> You run into that sort of thing: things that from your experience and knowledge of an area you think should be done, you feel certain should be done. For various reasons, the home office may decide not to do it. *That hurts sometimes.*

And another:

> If you are with people who are supportive and you have the right kind of financial backing, *it's a lot of fun to build an organization,* to put one together, to see it grow.

Embarrassment, hurt, fun? Not the cool, detached, professional manager of the stereotype. And because of this deep emotional involvement, problem recognition is often anything but a routine affair.

## My Reality or Yours?

In addition to the cognitive processes by which individual managers "create" problems, problems are also created interactively. Most managers spend most of their time interacting with other people, and the primary purpose of these conversations is to trade and process information.[56] Managers collaborate to determine what is "real." In the physical realm, people usually don't have a lot of trouble deciding what is real. Desks, machinery, and factories are demonstrably real, but it is not so simple to determine the meaning of the host of amorphous issues arising in organizations. Examples include judging what consumer response to a contemplated new product will be; determining whether an organization's career paths for upwardly mobile managers are laid out effectively; or deciding whether a multibillion dollar corporation should be decentralized further, and how. On vague and complex issues like these, managers interactively anchor their sense of reality. They validate their perceptions, opinions, and conclusions in conjunction with the people around them. Like all people, managers come to a common view by talking through the situation with others important to them and thereby achieve a narrowing and crystallizing of organizational reality.[57]

Not only is reality created interactively, it is negotiated—even contested—by the parties with a stake in the issue, and those parties with greater power stand a better chance of defining reality their way.

Problem recognition may be a contest between competing points of view backed up by different degrees of power, and managers sometimes manipulate the context to achieve political ends—even to the extent of keeping secrets and practicing deception.[58] An example of this occurred in the late sixties when certain Goodrich managers attempted to suppress test results indicating that aircraft brakes were faulty. At that time, the B. F. Goodrich Wheel & Brake Plant won a subcontract from Ling-Temco-Vought Co. to develop wheels and brakes for the Air Force A-7D plane. The brakes failed test after test, and the technical writer was given clear instructions to fudge the data. According to him, "many, many of the elaborate engineering curves attached to the report were complete and total fabrications, based not on what had actually occurred, but on information which would fool both LTV and the Air Force."[59] The technical writer, together with the laboratory staff that had conducted the tests, protested the fabrication of the data but was overruled. In a sense, the writer and lab staff were locked in a contest with their superiors over whether the negative results constituted a problem. Those with greater power won (for the time being).

If the person bringing a problem to a manager's attention is powerful, then the manager is likely to accept that person's definition. When, for example, higher management defines a need, ranging from a routine request to preparation of an elaborate plan or report, the manager is likely to accept the definition as given.[60]

Credibility is a kind of power, and the majority of managers interviewed by Lyles and Mitroff cited credibility as an important factor in determining whether an opinion carried weight. Together, rank and credibility make a great deal of difference in determining whether a person's view is accepted.[61]

The other side of the same coin is that those with low power in relation to the decision maker sometimes have trouble getting their views accepted. One chapter of the story of the DC-10 (cited in Chapter 1) is that the warnings of the safety experts about the faulty cargo door went largely unheeded.[62] More recently, engineers at Thiokol who opposed the shuttle launch were overruled by management.[63]

In another case, a refuse dump from a coal mine slid down into a village in England in 1966 and killed 144 people, including 109 children in school at the time. The local borough council had previously lodged a complaint to the British National Coal Board, pointing out that the refuse dump was dangerous, but, because the borough council was outside the coal industry, they had been dismissed as poorly informed and having little to contribute. One cause of disasters is that complaints and warnings from people outside the organization with jurisdiction over the situation are largely ignored.[64] The authorities can generally afford to disregard the complaints of outsiders, who typically lack any real power.

Thus, problem statements from powerful sources are likely to stick. But low-power sources will have trouble getting their views accepted and even more trouble getting action taken. Sometimes the power of sender and intended receiver is on a par, and the definition of the situation is worked out through negotiation and persuasion.

## CREATING PROBLEMS: AN OVERVIEW

Some problems are too new, or unexpected, to come to light routinely. These problems are "created"—in the sense that they emerge in the minds, emotions, and conversations of managers. This process, summarized in Figure 2-1, suggests that recognizing that problems exist is not an automatic part of the decision-making process. Formal systems, organizational structure, strong values, and managers' previous experience increase the probability that the information needed to identify routine, familiar problems will be available. But recognizing novel, unfamiliar, amorphous, or threatening problems is an entirely different matter. And it is precisely these kinds of problems for which managers, particularly at higher levels, must shoulder the responsibility. It is not enough to be aware of the perceptual blinders that we all wear and of the organiza-

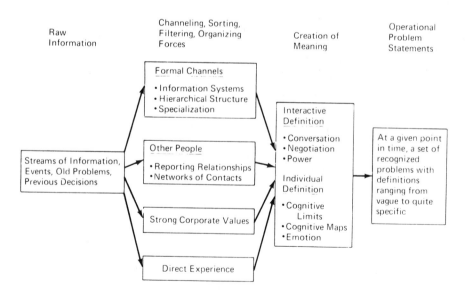

**Figure 2-1   The Process of Problem Creation**

tional forces that hinder information flow. Managerial action is required to compensate for these natural pitfalls. And given the sheer number of biases and distortions, it would be easy to accept paralysis. But the effective managers we've talked to are inveterate optimists—they don't spend much time dwelling on all the things that can go wrong or all the weaknesses of human beings. Rather, they move ahead, often acting intuitively, finding problems and solving them. They make plenty of mistakes, but they move past them quickly and often learn from them. As we examined their descriptions in detail, we found that what they called intuition had a behavioral base. There are things they *do* that have profound effects on how they gather information, process it, and put it together to "define" the problems they face. The two major themes that emerge—themes that will reappear consistently throughout this book—are *digging* and *knowing the business*. Specifically in reference to finding out what the problems are, we offer the following "advice from managers to managers":

## "Dig, Dig, Dig"

You dig with everybody. You listen to everybody. You've got to look at every interface with a human being as a potential for getting data, as an opportunity to learn something.

But as you dig and dig and dig and ask the right kinds of questions you begin to find there are basic errors in the way you do things.

If you dig into it enough and know enough about what you're doing, you can generally find out what the real problem is.

This composite description puts it in a nutshell. Without exception, the effective executives we talked to hammered home the theme of digging out the information. For virtually all significant issues, they abandoned the hierarchy, going directly to a worker, a superintendent, a customer, a supplier, a banker, a board member, a competitor—in one case, even the local bartender. These conversations were seldom restricted to a single problem or issue but almost always ranged widely across topics, as if the manager were a sponge soaking up information that at some future time might be of use. As one manager put it, "You only need one gem out of a thousand to really make it pay off."

There seem to be two behavioral features to digging: listening and asking questions. Listening, as described by managers, sounds very much like the "active listening" methods formulated by psychologists. Listening clearly involves more than the ears; it also involves the eyes ("watch the way a person gives you the data") and the mouth ("listening is repeating, repeat back what you heard"). Listening is not just understanding what is said but also understanding "what emotional condition the

YOU HAVE TO KNOW HOW TO DIG AND WHERE TO DIG.

speaker is saying it in. Is he upset? Is he afraid of you? Is he comfortable with me and the issue he's bringing to me?"

Anyone who has spent time with executives has seen the second behavioral manifestation of digging: the uncanny ability to ask questions. It's not the drill sergeant firing off questions (though most executives have to be good at this approach too), it's a much more subtle probing that doesn't activate defenses:

> I'll ask them enough questions to know whether they understand the subject they're talking about. That doesn't take too long, and you can do it in a way that doesn't even sound like you're checking. "By the way, how do you feel about such-and-such?" You can see right away if they know about it. But if you say, "Hey stupid, what makes you think you know anything about that?" that's the end of the input.

There seem to be a few intuitive rules effective managers follow while listening and asking questions. A cardinal rule, for example, is never to use what someone says to punish them. People who share bad news honestly may never do it again if it is used to hurt them. That's one reason many of these managers put so much effort into confirming—into using several different sources for the same information before acting on it.

The desire to "discuss things face to face" is almost an obsession with some executives. It's fine to have data and statistics and forecasts but not without that personal interaction. Nowhere was this more clearly exemplified than by one executive who reflected on formal presentations:

> I hate presentations. I like to talk about things. Let's *talk* about what we're going to do. When I first went to that plant, I'd ask a question and I'd get a

two-hour presentation with charts. I kept telling him, "I don't want all those charts. Just tell me, off the top of your head, how you feel about this. Christ, you've been in the job 30 years; you ought to know off the top of your head what's right or wrong." It took me a long time, but now I don't get presentations. We discuss things.

A major problem with this approach to "leading by listening" is that it can be very hard to cut it off. Once the environment is established, people like to talk, and any executive sociable enough to operate this way could spend all his or her time conversing.

## "You've Got to Know What You're Doing"

The key to running a company is to know as much as you possibly can about what your job is and the area you're working in and the product that you're selling and the people you have working for you.

There are two critical pieces to this second theme. The first is that you must know intimately the people you have to work with; otherwise, you can't dig effectively. Second, you've got to know the business cold, or else you don't know what to dig for or how to use what you learn.

The need to know people comes up repeatedly as executives talk about finding out what the problems are. Just as you have to dig with everybody, you have to know as many people as you can as well as you can. "I knew who was who and what they thought" is frequently at the core of effective managerial action. The "who" could be clients, customers, subordinates, superiors, bankers, competitors, suppliers, union representatives, or anyone else involved in the business. The "what they thought" includes their position on issues, their particular strengths and weaknesses, and, above all, what they could be depended upon to do.

This rather amazing (staggering?) array of contacts is not just wishful thinking or exaggeration. Recent research has documented that effective managers have hundreds and even thousands of contacts.[65]

Equally important to these executives was knowing the business. This was the primary way they had of making use of all they learned:

If you know your business, you know. You know what's important to keep it alive; you know where the really important things are. (And that just comes from being in the business long enough to really know it.) It's not just a surface kind of thing: it's knowing *why* something is important.

Knowing means the product, how it's made, how it's used, where it came from, what goes wrong with it, and just about every conceivable aspect of it. It's firsthand knowledge of all the significant aspects of what the manager manages.

Managers who know the people central to their business and the business itself have worked hard to get that knowledge. It is a product of years and years or even a whole career in the business.[66] But it is also the product of intensive effort by the manager to learn, a deliberate quest to know all there is to know. Particularly when a manager enters a new job, the priority agenda is getting to know the business and the people.[67] As one executive put it:

> Just as intensively as you can, you learn what's going on from whatever source you can. You spend as much time as you can doing that. You just budget your time, allow a little bit for sleep, and go on from there.

### "Know Yourself"

This bit of advice came not from a minister or psychologist but from the top human resources executive in a Fortune 100 company. He recommended self-knowledge not for its own sake but because of its eminently practical value for all aspects of management, including problem recognition. Those blinders, mental maps, biases, fears, hot buttons, and cherished beliefs that put a crimp in the information handling and processing of the people surrounding a manager also operate within the manager. While there is a limit to the ability of people to recognize deeply ingrained parts of themselves, the greater the perspective on oneself, the better one is in touch with one's world. We can't help having our personal needs and organizational interests distort our reading of situations, but we can work to minimize those distortions by being alive to those needs and interests.

An executive we interviewed, for example, who excelled in turning around subpar organizations, had a nose for what is wrong in any situation. He had to take into account the possibility that he would see problems that didn't exist or experience them as worse than they were. Another manager had a highly developed sense of order that made him an excellent systematizer and regularizer of the organizations he ran. Yet he needed to guard against having his perfectionist tendencies lead him to attend too much to organizational form and too little to substance.[68]

A basic characteristic that managers must recognize and ride herd on is their own defensiveness—their particular way of protecting themselves from threats to their self-esteem.[69] When the question of assigning responsibility arises, do they tend to take too little responsibility (or, for that matter, too much)? One manager we studied had a habit of defining his subordinates as personnel problems when, in fact, the difficulties inhered in his relationship with them; but his self-protective arrogance, combined with his superior position, allowed him to get away with pinning them with the blame. Another executive we studied exaggerated the importance of problems brought to his attention by higher-ups and had to break his habit of panicking at each imagined "crisis." At the root was his fear of looking bad in his superiors' eyes. Still another executive showed admirable self-awareness in telling us that he had to watch out for his reluctance to admit ignorance, an egotistical quirk that could keep him from fully understanding a problem.

Managers may prefer to see problems as lying outside of themselves, but the reality is that just as managers participate fully in disposing of problems, they are often bound up in the difficulties that result from the actions they take. They must be objective about themselves in relation to many of the external problems that arise.

## Bring an Open Mind

Managers work hard to develop their mental maps—of the business environment, their organizations, the people around them, themselves. But they must be ready and willing to revise or discard those maps, however time-honored or cherished, in the light of fresh experience. Just as they frame their experience, they must be able to reframe. Generalizing about professionals including managers, Schon observed that the individual should be "willing to step into the problematic situation, to impose a frame on it, . . . and yet to remain open to the situation's back-talk."[70] What is needed is managers with "minds that are attuned to existing patterns yet able to perceive important breaks in them."[71] The challenge is to know when to hold on to a pattern despite an occasional blip and when to let go of it in its present form in response to an instructive discontinuity. Managers eventually get themselves in trouble if they disregard early warning signals[72] or if, like an executive we spoke with, they are "quick to judge and slow to part with ironclad judgments."

Being open-minded requires that managers first of all pay attention when something unexpected happens. As Isenberg found, "Rather than deny, downplay, or ignore disconfirmation, successful senior managers often treat it as friendly and in a way cherish the discomfort surprise creates."[73] For managers to take this attitude, they must care more about continually learning than about preserving their image as knowledgeable. They must blend action and knowledge seeking as they make their way through the numerous episodes packed into each day. The better ones reflect on themselves in relation to the problems they grapple with, sometimes calling timeout and making that reflection explicit with the other parties to the problem.[74] To use this highly reflective approach to managing, which Torbert called "action inquiry," requires "a willingness to sacrifice your illusions about yourself, others, and situations as you receive new information."[75]

## In Conclusion

How, then, do problems get recognized? In organizational settings, meaning emerges as managers dig for information and interpret it against their knowledge of the business. In some cases, where contacts are good and knowledge is adequate, the problem is obvious. In other cases, only continual digging and reinterpretation, possibly coupled with false conclusions and inappropriate action, result in a clear understanding of the problem.

Interestingly, many of the formal mechanisms for channeling information and analyzing it are clearly of secondary importance—if not direct obstacles—to managers. Some are deliberately circumvented, particularly the hierarchy, and tenacious managers do not let specialization or functional allegiance deter their quest for meaning.

At any point in time, then, a manager's plate is overflowing with problems, ranging from those that are only vaguely defined to those that are quite specific. Of all these, which ones will get attention? The issue of priorities is the topic of the next chapter.

# 3

## *PRIORITIES*

## *FOR ACTION*

Leaders look forward to the future. They hold in their minds visions and ideals of what can be.[1]

To choose a direction, a leader must first have developed a mental image of a possible and desirable future state of the organization. This image, which we call a *vision,* may be as vague as a dream or as precise as a goal or mission statement.[2]

The agendas that these managers developed tended to be made up of a set of loosely connected goals and plans which addressed their long-, medium-, and short-run responsibilities. As such, the agendas typically addressed a broad range of financial, product/market, and organizational issues. They also included both vague and very specific items.[3]

Students of leadership have long argued that it is the leader's responsibility to set the direction for the organization. In the context of managerial decision making, it is tempting to believe that priorities are set by one's vision and leave it that. Whether an inspirational dream, a loosely formed agenda, or a set of inviolate values, what gets decided about and even the set of solutions available would seem to flow directly from the decision maker's sense of what should be.

Unfortunately, it is not enough to have a vision. The organizational context, the press of events, other people's agendas and visions, and a myriad of other forces come between what a manager may want to do and what he or she actually does. Even at the most pragmatic level, the fact that a problem exists doesn't mean that anyone will work on it. The following excerpt from Pounds is revealing:

> In a series of interviews, managers were asked to specify the problems currently faced by them and their organizations. Most of them mentioned from five to eight problems. Later in the same interview, each manager was asked to describe in broad terms his own activities for the previous week. In reviewing the data from these interviews as they were collected, it was noted that *no manager reported any activity which could be directly associated with the problems he had described.* [emphasis added][4]

This bit of irrational behavior found by Pounds is not at all irrational in view of the research on why certain problems get attention while others don't. Managers have more than enough to do, so they spend a great deal of their time responding to squeaky wheels. The fragmentation of manage-

rial work[5] is entirely compatible with the fragmentation of priorities and problems and with the constantly changing pressures for action. The actual importance of a given problem is likely the subject of debate: The pressure on a manager to do something about it is much more tangible.

One way to approach the material in this chapter is to say that the circumstances under which problems are most likely to get action have three basic elements. First, the manager must know there is a problem (which may be a disparity between an envisioned state and the current one) or, at the very least, must have a vague notion that something is wrong. Second, there must be some kind of pressure for the manager to act, such as a deadline, a crisis, or an expectation from the boss. Third, the manager must have, or be able to obtain, the resources necessary to take action (resources being broadly defined as authority, information, expertise, money, and so on). The relationship of the three elements to probability of action is shown in Figure 3-1. The reality of managerial action is depicted by Cell 0, the intersection of problems, pressure, and resources. To gain some control over the problems worked on, a manager must know how to manipulate all three elements.

Consider, for example, the situation suggested in Cell 1, where a problem is recognized and the manager has the resources to act, but there is no external pressure. The research suggests that this is the domain of the "back burner": problems a manager thinks are important and ought to get action, but continually get put off. Somehow problems with external pressure keep shunting these problems aside, and that is one of the

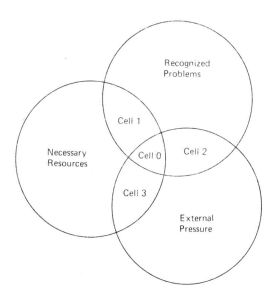

**Figure 3-1   Where the Action Is**

reasons that visions, agendas, and good intentions aren't always enough by themselves.

The manager wanting to see action on back-burner problems must somehow move them to Cell 0. One obvious way to do this is to create external pressure. Edison, for example, is said to have scheduled a press conference when he was stalled over a problem. This created a deadline and forced the process forward. There are many ways to create pressure for action on a problem: allocate funds for it, find an external client, promise the boss, make it highly visible.

Another option for Cell 1 problems is to delegate them, with the manager then becoming the external pressure for the subordinate. The key here is for the manager to be sure the subordinate knows what the problem is and can get the resources to act.

Other problems not likely to get action can be found in Cell 2, where there are recognized problems and pressure to act, but the manager does not have the resources to act. This is a large and familiar domain for most of us, especially since few people have all the resources they need (or think they need) to act on an important problem. Managers in staff positions know this domain well, as they are often under pressure to act but lack the authority to make other people do things. Lower level managers are also familiar with this cell: the boss asking for another miracle.

The director of a corporate contributions program found himself in this predicament when senior management decided to expand the contributions program by a factor of three. The *problem* was there: the need to improve the corporation's public image and to win the good will of the communities where corporate facilities were located. The *pressure* was there: both top management and the board of directors had mandated a stepped-up contributions effort and had tripled the money set aside for it—money that had to be spent. What the contributions director lacked at first were the *resources* to implement the expansion. He had too few people available to work on the program, a shortage of expertise in the area, and a dearth of ideas on how to spend the money fruitfully. To move on this, he had to find and develop these missing resources.

Like the corporate contributions director, the managers facing Cell 2 problems do have options for reaching Cell 0. They can try to get the necessary resources directly (for example, requesting a budget variance); hand the problem over to someone else who has the resources (this may require redefining the problem so that it is central to someone else); or, through negotiation, bargaining, and coalitions, gain access to needed resources.

Cell 3, the case of a manager with resources and under pressure to use them but without a recognized problem, is more subtle. Cohen and March have described this domain as solutions in search of a problem.[6] A manager who is under budget should be delighted, but in many cases next year's budget will be cut unless this year's funds are expended. Suddenly, managerial effort must be invested in finding worthy problems in which to invest resources.

Cell 3 is a common one for research and development, where products are not always tangible. Basic research can take years to pay off, but there is often pressure for R&D to justify itself because of the amount of resources tied up in personnel and equipment. Managers then find themselves in a position of creating problems for which basic research or intermediate results might be the solution. The March of Dimes ran into this kind of obstacle when Jonas Salk developed polio vaccine and achieved the organization's original mission of raising funds to find a cure for polio. The March of Dimes filled the void by redirecting its fund-raising capacity toward another child-related health problem, birth defects.[7]

Options in Cell 3 include reducing the pressure or generating problems. One way to reduce pressure is to buy time with promises of delivery at a future date. This strategy will go only so far and increases the pressure as the deadline approaches.

Another option is to find or generate interesting problems somehow related to what you are doing. One of the arts of managing R&D, for example, is showing higher level, nontechnical managers how the research is helping solve *their* problems.

According to this broad-brush analysis, managerial action will not occur unless all three ingredients are present—problems, resources, and pressure. In what follows we assume a problem exists, that it has been recognized, and we offer a finer grained discussion of the forces affecting whether a manager will work on it or not.

## TO ACT OR NOT TO ACT

Obviously, being aware that problems exist, and even having some idea of their relative importance, does not tell us what managers will do. As the last chapter showed, information can be treated in such ways that problems do not get recognized at all. It also suggested that managers have more than enough problems to stay busy. This section deals with how managers decide whether or not to *act*, given that they know there is a problem.

When managers decide whether to work on problems and in what order, they are, in effect, assigning priorities. Consciously or unconsciously, managers set their own agenda for the present and future. They pick and choose among the wide array of possible tasks in front of them—tasks consisting not just of problems that need fixing but opportunities that invite exploiting. This steady succession of items, small and large, comes from the people around the manager but can also be self-generated. Because so much is thrown at them, managers are all inevitably in a reactive mode—and some prefer it, fielding things one after another like

JUST BECAUSE A PROBLEM EXISTS DOESN'T MEAN
THAT SOMEONE WILL WORK ON IT.

people playing attack-type video games. Other managers take a proactive approach, driven by their short- and long-range agendas.[8] As they make their way through the thicket of daily events, these managers practice a kind of opportunism, converting the reactive mode into a chance to move proactively on their own, often larger, agendas.[9]

What managers choose to work on, how they spend their time and energy, is absolutely basic. "Life in business, or otherwise, is fundamentally a matter of attention."[10] How managers focus attention, their own and that of others, is a crucial part of decision making.[11]

### The Choice of Inaction

It is not clear from the research what proportion of recognized problems are deliberately ignored or avoided by managers, but it has been suggested that it is large.[12] For any number of reasons, managers seem to respond to problematic situations by waiting, perhaps hoping that many of these situations will go away on their own accord. In many cases this may be a viable strategy: Thomas reports that 35 percent of patients with rheumatoid arthritis are bound to recover no matter what the doctor does.[13] We don't know what the spontaneous recovery rate for managerial problems is, but if it even approaches 35 percent, ignoring problems is an attractive option. In an organizational context, Clark and Shrode found that many problems do, in fact, go away, often by becoming someone else's.[14]

One reason for putting off action on problems is that it is often difficult to know what one is getting into. Problematic situations are often only vaguely understood at the start,[15] decision opportunities are often ambiguous,[16] and it is often hard to estimate the significance of a particular problem.[17] This uncertainity is enhanced because individual managers have only limited influence on what the organization decides its problems are.[18]

In short, many problems represent a Pandora's box for managers who can't be sure how much time, energy, or trouble may lie ahead once a particular problem gets their attention. Even when the parameters of a problem become clear, as they usually do once the problem-solving process gets underway, there are often decided advantages in stalling and buying time[19] and in avoiding commitments.[20]

Not the least of the forces encouraging delay in attacking fuzzy problems is the danger of hurting the "track record." Numerous studies have shown the importance of a manager's credibility to his or her ability to get things done,[21] and much of that credibility comes from past successes in problem solving. Where the nature of a problem is unclear, the consequences of bungling suggest caution. Just as managers are likely to assign greater weight to losses than to gains,[22] they are likely to be circumspect about working on (and thus owning) a problem before they have some idea that it can be solved successfully. In short, it is often wise to have one's ducks in a row before becoming identfied with action on a problem.

Managers also delay action on a problem for not-so-good reasons. The big, amorphous, and perplexing problems make managers uneasy, and some managers succumb to the temptation to procrastinate. When managers complain that they're so busy they can't get into the important issues, the real reason may be different. Rather than tackle the tough items on their dockets, managers sometimes keep themselves comfortable by keeping busy.[23] In cases like these, the manager's heavy load and high activity level take a bum rap.

Another factor that negates action is vested interest. Investment in the status quo delayed DuPont's exit from the manufacture of black powder in the first years of this century. Alfred I. DuPont, one of the three family members running the company, had grown up in this longstanding DuPont business and "was wedded to black powder and passionately fond of the process, as well as the men who mixed and milled and glazed it."[24]

Likewise, the next technological breakthrough doesn't tend to occur in those companies with huge amounts of capital tied up in the last generation of technology. "The mechanical typewriter manufacturers did not introduce the electric typewriter; the electric typewriter people did not invent the electronic typewriter; vacuum tube companies did not introduce the transistor, and so on."[25] In the early seventies, Xerox, with 95 percent of the world's market for copiers captured, had a chance to develop the first personal computer years ahead of Apple and IBM. But preoccupied with its single highly successful product, the company's management rejected the proposal of its researchers in California to complete development of its years-ahead technology.[26] For the same reason that it is "never the industry leader that makes the big leap"[27] managers sitting pretty in their organizations may develop conservative tendencies. One forty-eight-year-old executive who had just vaulted to a vice-presidency in another corporation recognized that his management style wasn't all it could be but said he wasn't about to risk his highly prized position. "My management style got me this far and I'm not about to tinker with it." This executive's stake in what he had achieved made him conservative about change.

Another factor that leads to inaction is poor relationships at work. Because a relationship in this condition lacks the reciprocity that leads to mutual responsiveness,[28] managers on bad terms with a coworker may drag their feet when asked to do something. By withholding cooperation, these managers delay action or stop it altogether.

So for a whole host of reasons, some good and some not so good, managers sometimes respond to problems by stalling. Managers have room to maneuver, and they use the latitude to stall, to deflect, to hold at bay. They will avoid a problem until the time is right, until the problem goes away, or until it is sufficiently well defined to make the consequences of attacking it reasonably clear. Despite the no-action option, however, problems do get solved and decisions do get made. As we will see, action on problems is expected of managers, both as a matter of course and as a result of pressures.

### The Choice to Act: Day-to-Day Administration

Problems arrive in no particular order[29] and, in the absence of pressure, tend to be handled sequentially on their own merits.[30] This "first in, first out" tendency is even reflected in the common time management advice to managers, "Never handle a piece of paper more than once." It is, after all, the function of organizational structure to channel problems to certain places, and doing the work requested is often less trouble than questioning the request.[31] The present-focused, take-them-as-they-come nature of managerial activities is well documented by diary and observational studies of managerial work,[32] and there is no reason to believe that the sequence of tackling problems should be any different.

Managers, of course, are not automatons; they use judgement in choosing what things to decide. Personal judgment is a major theme in the research on decision making,[33] and it seems logical that, given a choice, managers will work on problems that seem reasonable to work on. Unsullied by other forces, the choice of what to act on would be guided by a manager's vision or agenda or, in certain situations, by values.[34] Personal judgments about what should be worked on do not emerge simply from within, however. There are at least four general areas identified in

PROBLEMS ARRIVE IN NO PARTICULAR ORDER.

the research that affect personal judgments: instructions, ownership, availability of solutions, and context.

A manager who is instructed to solve a certain problem (usually by someone at a higher level) is likely to do so. Problem definitions and problem-solving instructions strongly influence problem solving,[35] and by inference these same factors are likely to influence the choice of which problems to work on. Instructions are likely to define the problem for a manager and therefore relieve him or her of the responsibility for deciding what the problem is and whether or not action should be taken. In effect, the manager accepts someone else's judgment of what the problem is and that it is important enough to work on. As one executive said, "One thing about priorities is the question 'what does the boss want?' "

Managers also get instructions at a more general level, guidelines that affect what they choose to work on. A department head who had worked closely with the executive director of a hospital for several years said that they regularly discussed the larger issues facing the organization:

> From discussing various things going on in the hospital or outside the hospital, I usually have a pretty good idea of what we are and where we're going. From that I don't get marching orders. I just have an array of issues in my mind that may come up the next day or next year. A tickler file, so to speak.

In taking their cues from their boss and others at higher levels, managers pay more attention to what higher-ups do than what they say—to what *they* actually spend time on. "Their action expresses their priorities."[36] If a manager's boss says he cares about quality but his actions reveal an indifference to it, then the manager won't give quality much importance. Managers will be guided by the theories that they superiors actually follow, not those that they merely espouse.[37]

Managers are also likely to consider issues of problem ownership when deciding what problems to attack. Other things being equal, managers are reluctant to encroach on another manager's turf. A manager is not likely to go about solving a problem when another manager is more directly affected by the consequences of the decision.[38] One's position in the organization influences perception of the problem,[39] and managers are quite predictably discreet when a problem is clearly within someone else's domain. Managers, like the rest of us, would just as soon avoid entanglement in a political morass. By the same token, managers are likely to act first on problems clearly within their own domain of responsibility, especially when their responsibility for other problems is unclear.

The availability of solutions is another factor likely to influence managerial problem choice. Managers seem to prefer problems that they can put bounds on, that can be reduced to simpler problems.[40] The decision-making research has shown that people prefer to use simple strategies to solve problems[41] and that managers using simple problem-solving strategies are in fact judged successful by their organization.[42] A reasonable manager, then, will tend to work on problems for which there are simple solutions and preferably for which solutions are in the immediate neighborhood of the problem.[43] In other words, managers are prone to act more quickly on problems that look easy to solve and procrastinate over tackling issues that are ambiguous.[44]

Managerial choice of problems is clearly influenced by the swirl of things around them—the context in which problems are embedded. There are certain elements that guide many organizational choices, such as established levels of acceptable risk or minimum expected return,[45] and problems that do not lend themselves to analysis using clear parameters are less likely to be tackled.

Context also includes corporate values—what the organization treats as important. Effective organizations adopt selected values or priorities, which effectively channel the attention and energies of the large body of organization members—for example, IBM's overriding concern with customer service, respect for people, and technical excellence.[46] One executive told us:

> A priority gets set if something happens that seems to upset one of the traditions of the company. [This company] prides itself on being quality. So if there's anything that interferes with quality, that becomes a priority. You pull people off other things, find out what the problem is, and correct it.

One of the most pervasive contextual factors in problem selection is the history of a problem. A problem seen historically as being in someone else's domain or as a hot potato or as being intractable is less likely (in the absence of external pressure) to get action than one that either is free of historical context or is an old friend. Managers are particularly prone to act on problems similar to problems they have solved successfully in the past. Historical context also applies to relationships: If problem solving is likely to require interaction with people with whom the problem solver has worked successfully in the past, action is more likely.

Managerial choice is affected not only by conditions outside the manager but by the manager's own preferences as well. An executive told us:

> Priorities get set because of your own interest in a particular thing. [As corporate director of personnel], I was interested in labor relations so I spent a lot of time on that. I was interested in compensation and benefits so I spent quite a bit of time on that.

The chance to express preferences in one's job increases with the latitude afforded by the job. Latitude generally increases at higher levels, in flexible environments, and in newly created jobs where there is no clear direction.[47] Managers can also find room to move in the spaces between their turf and others' turf. One manager explained:

> There is a lot of work to be done that no one else is interested in doing. You can expand your domain without treading on anyone's toes.[48]

In summary, when there are no external pressures operating, managers tend to act on problems sequentially and to act on problems for which definitions, problem-solving strategies and rules, and/or the likelihood of success are reasonably clear. These general tendencies do not preclude acting on a few problems just because a manager thinks they are important. But the forces at work in managerial jobs make it easy to be reactive and self-protective.

In the day-to-day routine of managerial life, then, general problem-solving tendencies and personal priority setting are important factors in determining what problems get attention. But, as we all know, external pressures of various kinds constantly upset the routine. The occurrence of a crisis, for example, will divert managers and resources from other problems.[49] Scarcity of resources can change everything; the routine of budgeting can be transformed by cutbacks into a major problem.

## Managers under Pressure: There's Always Something

External pressures frequently override the take-it-as-it-comes approach to decision making. Pressures that determine problem priority come in many forms, including deadlines, crises, other people's activities, previous commitments, and accidents.

Research has shown that managers often work first on problems that are likely to get worse.[50] Research has also shown that the current press gets the attention,[51] or as James put it, "What holds attention determines action."[52] Perhaps the most frequent priority setters are ever-present deadlines.[53] In a fascinating review of research on deadlines, Webb and Weick showed that as a deadline approaches, there is a dramatic increase in activity. (This is true in a variety of settings and regardless of the amount of time prior to the deadline.)[54] Even in research tracing decision making over time, the last period before final choice contains markedly more activity.[55] This suggests that managers, constantly juggling many different problems, pay increasing attention to certain problems as the deadline for action approaches. In some cases deadlines may be directly established, as in a contract delivery date, or they may be more indirect, as in a scheduled meeting for project authorization. The point is that a world containing many problems crying for attention will also be a world of deadlines—some problems will come first simply because they must.

Another major source of problem priorities is crisis. In an interview about a typical day, the president of a small company remarked that an average day contained three of four crises,[56] each of which called for quick action. A crisis may be a sudden event, such as the unexpected cutoff of a raw material, or it may result from letting things slide for so long that a problem can no longer be ignored.[57]

When we asked one executive how he set priorities, he said:

Well, the first thing is that a crisis gets attention. There's no question that when the price of [a commodity essential to his manufacturing organization] went through the roof, what do to about it immediately commanded

attention. If you have an explosion in the plant, you immediately act. That's not really a decision that an individual makes; the decision is made for him and he reacts.

Because crises occur on a regular basis, managers have to be prepared to adjust their priorities. One executive put it this way:

You can't set any firm priorities for too long a time. Things change and you just have to revise your priorities as you go along. When an emergency comes up, you have to shelve everything and get on that.

Ian Mitroff and his colleagues at the Center for Crisis Management at the University of Southern California have identified many types of disasters with potentially devastating consequences for an organization (a partial listing of which appears below). Any of these events could instantly override any other source of managerial priorities:

- major product defects
- major plant/equipment defects
- major industrial accidents
- major computer breakdowns
- hostile takeovers
- sabotage/product tampering
- counterfeiting
- false rumors, malicious slander
- bribery, price fixing
- sexual harassment
- terrorism, executive kidnapping
- recalls
- boycotts
- loss of proprietary information[58]

It is apparent, then, that people who want total control over their work life will not like managing.

If crises and deadlines account for many problem priorities, still more are accounted for by other people in the organization. As Pounds's study pointed out, other people's problems tend to become your problems, and other people's solutions to their problems can become your problems.[59] Examples of the former are inherent in the tendency of managers to ignore problems; when they "go away," it is likely that they have gone to someone else. If marketing does not generate clients, production may develop an inventory problem. On the other hand, when production gets rid of its deadwood by transferring them to personnel, that can create a new array of problems for personnel.

In addition to having to deal with what other people discard or ignore, managers are actively recruited to become involved in other people's problems and projects. Pressure in this form arises when opportunity knocks. Innovation is one such opportunity, and managers may find themselves being recruited to work on a project team or, if they are at high levels, to fund the project. In either case, pressure is applied to the managers to own a piece of the problem. "Product champions" are often the carriers of these opportunities. Just as innovation won't happen without them ("our project almost didn't happen when X left the company and there was nobody left to drive it"), product champions can't launch or complete projects without a lot of help. Because of their dependent plight, product champions go after help aggressively. Tom West, the inspirational and enigmatic manager who oversaw the development of a new generation of computers at Data General, spoke of "signing on" new recruits as if they were being inducted into a secret society.[60] Another powerful carrier of opportunities is the customer. Evidence shows that the better companies allow new product development to be guided, or even to be initiated, by their customers. IBM has been successful technologically by responding to the needs of its leading customers, whereas NCR fell behind in the late sixties when it declined to meet its leading customers' demands for advanced electronics.[61] In effect, the better companies practice a form of good listening. They allow their customers to apply pressure and to shape their priorities.

A fourth general source of pressure is commitment to a course of action that is failing. Failure is a general sensitizer[62] and causes people to seek more information and scrutinize more carefully before acting. That managers sometimes throw good money after bad has been established in a series of laboratory studies,[63] and they do so for a variety of reasons. Among them are personal commitment through previous decisions and the degree of threat implied by visibility to other, higher ranking decision makers. Thus, a manager faced with failure after a series of visible decisions will likely choose to work on problems that might salvage those earlier decisions.[64]

Priorities also get set by chance. Accidents can create commitment to action on problems. An example of this was the decision in World War II to require unconditional surrender of all Axis powers. This controversial decision, some argue, prolonged the war by driving the enemy to desperation. Yet it was made more or less by accident. Here is Churchill's account of how the decision was made at the Casablanca Conference in January of 1943:

> It was with some feeling of surprise that I heard the President say at the Press Conference on January 24 that we would enforce "unconditional surrender" upon all our enemies. . . . In my speech which followed the President's I of course supported him and concurred in what he had said. Any divergence between us, even by omission, would on such an occasion and at such a time have been damaging or even dangerous to our war effort. . . .

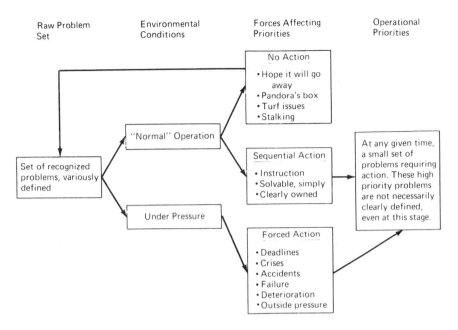

**Figure 3-2    Setting Action Priorities**

And here is the president's account to [Harry] Hopkins:

> We had so much trouble getting those two French generals together that I thought to myself that this was as difficult as arranging a meeting of Grant and Lee—and then suddenly the Press Conference was on, and Winston and I had had no time to prepare for it, and the thought popped into my mind that they had called Grant "Old Unconditional Surrender," and the next thing I knew I had said it.[65]

In summary (see Figure 3-2), sequential decision making tempered by judgment is easily and frequently replaced by the need for managerial action in response to pressure, other people, pressing opportunities, failing commitments, and accidents.

## WHAT TO WORK ON: SOME WORDS OF ADVICE

Operating within a set of constraints, managers pick and choose among an unending series of demands, many of them imposed from the outside, some of them self-imposed. As to whether they accept or reject a problem, and as to how they attend to it if they choose to, they have varying degrees of choice.[66] How much choice depends on who they are and what position they occupy as well as the nature of the problem.

From our interviews with managers and our reading of the literature come a few rules of thumb to guide the manager through the thicket. Much of this advice may at first seem contradictory. How, after all, can one "do it now" and "do it later"? The contradictions evaporate when one considers the ever-changing landscape of decisions and the constant tensions between short and long term, between personal goals and external pressures. The central challenge to the manager is what Isenberg calls "strategic opportunism," defined as "the ability to remain focused on long-term objectives while staying flexible enough to solve day-to-day problems and recognize new opportunities."[67] Thus, action on one problem or part of a problem may appear to contradict another action unless one considers the larger context of what a manager is trying to accomplish and what exigencies must be taken into account. As one of the executives Isenberg studied described it:

> Sometimes I feel like a rhinoceros who doesn't see well and whose power of concentration is terrible; he charges at something that's a long way off, then forgets where he is going and stops to eat grass.[68]

## Do It Now

As discussed earlier, there are times when a crisis lands in the manager's lap and the decision about whether to attend to the problem is automatic. Or at least it seems to be. In terms of the model presented at the beginning of this section, this is a case in which *external pressure* to act on a *recognized problem* is so great that the manager somehow finds the *necessary resources* to deal with the problem. One executive explained:

> Some things just have to be handled quickly or else the whole organization could go down the drain. If you get something like that you have to do whatever it takes right away. You learn from experience what is most serious when problems arise.

In assessing the urgency of a situation, managers can overreact or underreact. As this executive indicated, experience is an important teacher in helping the individual accurately gauge the seriousness of a situation. Asked how you know a vital interest is being threatened, another executive said, without hesitation: "If you know your business, you know."

### Do It Later

Managers delay action when it is clear to them they can't solve the problem by acting on it now. Managers practice the art of the possible and studiously avoid situations in which the resistance to an initiative would be prohibitively high. As one manager put it, "I deliberately procrastinate on some things. Those are the situations where, if you push, you're making a big mistake." This is a case in which not all the necessary resources—that is, the receptiveness of key constituents—are present to justify responding to the pressure to act on a problem.

A good sense of timing also seems all-important. Talking about how he learned to deal with resistance below, one manager in a medical setting said:

> If there's one lesson I have learned it's timing. You can just beat your head against a brick wall. . . . It's a problem that many physicians have in a medical setting because they're accustomed to taking definitive action.

Another manager who prided himself on his ability to influence people counseled nevertheless:

> It is extremely important to be patient, to realize that time will take its course on some things and, no matter what you do, things are going to play themselves out. . . . You've got to look at the effect of time on decision making.

Evident here is a certain philosophical attitude: As an alternative to forcing an unpopular issue, the manager can engage in something called "systematic waiting."[69]

## Do It Sooner

In addition to responding to pressing problems, managers are quite capable of acting on a problem *before* it becomes full-blown. The principle is: Act now and save yourself bigger trouble later. Advised one executive:

> You try to make a decision before the data gets to the point where the data makes the decision for you. You step in and anticipate. You see the trend and, say "All right, I've got to do something before suddenly the data says it for me."

A hospital administrator talked about how he anticipated that the method by which hospitals are reimbursed would change:

> I played a hunch and I said: "This is something that's going to happen and it's really going to blow us out of the water if we don't do something." And there are now more and more people who are beginning to realize that there is a drastic change in the way that hospitals operate.

Instead of being galvanized into action by a crisis, these managers try to head off a problem before it reaches crisis proportions. But it is harder to get yourself and others to work on a *potential* problem. One executive agonized over the fact that his division's fortunes might suffer:

> We've done some great things and I continually have this sense that my people are kind of coasting ("We're making all this money," they say), and I'm scared stiff. The way I characterize it to them is that I feel like we're in a boat going down a rapid river and I know there's a big, rock-filled waterfall down there. I'm the only one who knows it's there and if we don't do something about it, we're going to get killed. . . .
> It's very typical of American managers—they do very well in a crisis. . . . But wouldn't it be nice if we did the things before we got to the crisis?

Again, in terms of our three-part model, managers are sometimes threatened with postponing action on a problem because, although resources are potentially available, the pressure to act is not present. Can managers create the pressure to act now by feeling keenly the seriousness of a problem that might develop later?

## Do Two Things at Once

Perpetually overloaded, managers are constantly on the alert for efficiencies. For this reason they are never happier than when they can kill two (or more) birds with one stone. Here the manager responds to the pressure to act on multiple problems by drawing on a single set of resources. One manager expressed it this way:

> What you're really looking for as a manager is: Can I make one decision and attack two problems? If I can do that, then I can marshall my resources in a way that I can be much more productive. So that sometimes determines my priorities.

A related kind of opportunism is when managers use a specific problem as a vehicle for raising the basic issue that the problem represents. One executive told us: "My attitude is that all problems are generic." Another executive told us that when he went to the CEO for authorization to buy a new computer (price tag, $700,000), he used the occasion to bring up the company's long-term data-processing needs. A mundane kind of efficiency is the common managerial practice of using every encounter, including impromptu conversations in the hall, as a chance to work on one of their agendas.[70] This opportunistic attitude is evident in the statement that one executive made: "You've got to look at every interface with a human being as a potential for gathering data, an opportunity to learn something."

## Do It Anyway

Most managers employ some decision rule, tacit or explicit, for which items they shunt to subordinates and which ones they work on themselves.[71] Although most of what gets shunted is accepted routinely, the manager on the receiving end sometimes has trouble with an item. Then, if the superior won't budge, the question becomes: Fight or accept defeat gracefully. One executive framed the issue as follows:

> If he wants a 10 percent cut in personnel because that happens to be what he wants, that may not be the right thing to do now from a business standpoint, but if that's what he wants you to give it to him. My people may not like some of these things, but we've got to do it, because if I don't do those things, I won't get what I really want. You have to lose some small battles to win the big ones. . . . Now there are some things they ask for that will destroy the business and then you've got to get tough.

It is clear that managers think twice before refusing to accept a directive.

When managers have to turn around and relay instructions they don't like, they may find themselves in a quandary. But the managers we interviewed stressed the importance of taking ownership of that piece of business. One executive felt strongly that:

> The worst way to communicate to an organization is to say, "We're doing this because the boss wants us to." Good managers will define it in their

terms. You have to accept ownership of the problem and redefine it to get the organization working on it. You've got to make it your priority, your problem.

Another executive gave similar advice:

> So when he says you have to do it in such a way, you find the positive sides of what he wants you to do, and then you build that up with your troops: "Sure, there are negative things but let's remember now there are a lot of good things about doing this."

This posture toward unwelcomed agendas puts a premium on loyalty and flexibility.

## Do It Your Way

Effective managers react to what is thrown at them but also use the latitude available to them and the power at their disposal to create their own agendas. They take the initiative in recognizing problems and in creating the pressure and finding the resources to solve them. When the agenda is strategic, it provides the manager with a perspective that determines which problems get attention. An executive quoted earlier set himself the task of worrying about the future: "What are we going to do to survive, long term? That's our most critical problem." A university dean related how he took it upon himself to spearhead an attempt to win federal funds for a major research center, one of only a dozen to be established nationally:

> Nobody told me we would have the research center here. In fact, the administrator I report to didn't support the idea. . . . So because it wasn't a high priority for him, I took it on myself. It was clear to me that it was a high priority for the university because there was heavy stress on this on the national scene. If you buck-passed on this one, it would hurt you institutionally. It would hurt the prestige. You would lose a lot of luster for other funding. Also I was comfortable with the legislative process; I thought we could win this one.

Proactive managers set their own agendas, whether specific and short run or abstract and long run.[72] One high-level manager described how he and his boss, the top person, set direction for themselves and the organization:

> He and I go out to Wendy's and have a hamburger and just kind of throw things off the wall and whatever bounces off is something that I will begin to take the initiative on. These things start out as blue-sky but you'd be surprised, because this field is changing so quickly, how many of them bear fruit and become very important.

Effective managers, in conjunction with the people around them, fashion their own programs for themselves and their organizations.[73] Their agendas run the gamut from people to products, from next month to next year and beyond. Agendas vary greatly as to how well defined, explicit, and conscious they are, and agendas are constantly forming and precipitating out as managers constantly encounter their worlds. The fifteen general managers whom Kotter studied started their jobs with only a vague notion, based on their acquaintance with the organization and the business, as to what their agendas were. But in their first several months on the job, the GMs formed their agendas for the short and long run through an elaborate, continuous process of gathering information and shaping plans. Out of this searching and sifting came a loose and often unwritten configuration of goals, plans, and projects.[74]

## Experiment with New Ways

As discussed, it is easy as an organization pushes hard to establish and maintain a line of business for that business to become entrenched to the point where it can't be fundamentally revamped and where possibilities for new businesses get crowded out.[75] It is incumbent on managers to take an experimental attitude toward both established products and services (they're not sacred) and those with uncertain potential (they may be the wave of the future). Somehow managers must find the happy medium between maintaining stability and introducing change. Just as it doesn't help to be a stick-in-the-mud, it is no help to the organization for a manager to make changes willy-nilly.[76] One variable regulating the balance of stability and change is the composition of the management team: Younger managers and those with fewer years of experience in the firm are more likely to innovate and take risks, while older managers with longer tenure in the organization are more likely to respect and conserve an organization's traditions.[77]

There is something fundamentally important in these parodoxical bits of advice. It isn't enough to have a compelling vision of what could be. It isn't enough to be an effective gunslinger, reacting with lightning speed to whatever pops up. The true artistry in managing an agenda is the ability to combine the two: to progress, however haltingly, toward the larger ends while at the same time handling well all the unexpected and necessary detours. Even more demanding may be working the bits and pieces of the day to day so that they eventually add up to the larger vision.

So, while visions may burst forth in all their glory, the agendas that guide priorities don't emerge full-blown from the heads of managers; they emerge gradually from their experience. Plans are outcroppings of action as much as action crops up from plans. The next two sections will describe how problems, once they are chosen for action, actually get resolved.

# 4

# *INTO ACTION*

We do
not what we wish, but what we can.[1]

In a rational world, simple, low magnitude problems would be dispensed with quickly and directly, while complex, high magnitude problems would receive the full treatment. We would expect to see a continuum of possible action types ranging from the very simple and direct to the very convoluted and lengthy. In fact, we do see such a continuum. There are many routine problems to be dealt with, and there are quick and direct ways of dealing with them. There are also complex problems to be solved, and complex, convoluted means for solving them are available. The rub is this: There is only a mild association between the type of problem—from simple to complex—and the type of action required by the problem. Simple problems are not always dealt with by simple means; complex problems are not always subjected to complex, convoluted action.

There is a broad class of problems of high complexity, ambiguity, and substantial risk that are nonetheless usually dealt with quickly and directly. Perhaps the most common of these is the so-called "fix-it." These require swift response to prevent disruption of the work flow or serious damage to the business. Calling in a million-dollar note, the sudden cancellation of vital insurance, unexpected cost overruns, and equipment breakdown are all examples in which the failure to act quickly can have dire consequences. Yet all of these are likely to be highly complex problems. Another problem of this type involves the sudden emergence of opportunities that, if not quickly seized, can evaporate. Grabbing a chance to break into a new market, being offered an unexpectedly good price on equipment you do not need at the moment, or putting together a catch-up deal to beat the competition; all represent fleeting opportunities that require quick action, even though the issues involved may be quite complicated and risky. There are other examples: Intervening when a poor decision has been made by someone else in the organization requires speed in the face of complexity; authorizing a subordinate's request for action in urgent circumstances can be a virtual act of faith, considering the complexities that may be involved.

The reverse of these examples can also occur. Matters that should be routine sometimes refuse to behave routinely. The assignment of company parking spaces, for example, is frequently anything but simple. As we shall see in the next section, the presence of powerful conflicting interests can draw out a decision to agonizing lengths. Sometimes it does not matter that the issue is relatively trivial.

If the type of action required by problems is not necessarily related to the type of problem instigating the action, what *does* affect whether action on a problem will be quick and direct or lengthy and convoluted? In many, if not all, instances it is the context in which the problem arises.

## CONTEXTUAL FACTORS AFFECTING THE TYPE OF ACTION

Some managers are more or less natural "hip-shooters"; they have a proclivity for quick, decisive action in a wide variety of circumstances. Other managers are naturally cautious and prefer to study problems carefully, even fairly routine problems, before acting. Certainly, these individual preferences can influence the kind of action a problem receives. But if we assume that most managers at least try to approach problems rationally, giving a problem no more and no less than it deserves, we find that there are certain contextual factors that strongly affect whether action will be swift and sure or drawn out and convoluted.

### The Urgency of the Problem

Perhaps the single most important contextual factor is urgency. The pressure of an impending deadline can override all other factors. Even the most complex problem, one that might normally lead to a lengthy and complicated decision-making process, will be resolved quickly if enough time pressure is applied to it. As one manager put it, "Some things just have to be handled quickly or the whole company will go down the drain. . . . You have to do whatever it takes right away." Such a deadline is an example of real urgency. But urgency can also be fabricated. It can be created by a boss, by a customer, by anyone who hopes to speed things up by saying, "I need it yesterday." So, urgency is not always what it appears to be. Sometimes a problem is seen as being urgent when only a part of the problem requires immediate action, while the rest of it can be taken care of in good time. And, like time itself, urgency is relative. Depending on the magnitude of the problem involved, a two-week deadline could be either cause for panic or a chance for a ten-day vacation. The point is this: It is someone's *perception* of the degree of urgency that affects the kind of action that will be applied to a problem. Perceived urgency can obviate any or all of the factors discussed next and lead to quick action, no matter how complex the problem may be.

### How the Problem Is Defined

After urgency, the next most important factor may be how a problem is defined. As we have seen earlier, problems are what a manager makes of them. Since managers "create" the problems they face, they can choose to define them in any of numerous ways. Some of these definitions will lead to quick action.

Managers may choose to see or define a problem as being simple, or sometimes they simplify a problem to deal with it. As one said, "I don't understand complicated problems. I only understand simple ones."[2] Sometimes managers unintentionally simplify a problem by mistaking a piece of the problem for the whole or a symptom for a cause. Such simplifications can lead to simplified—and quick—responses. Managers can also choose to define a problem so that it fits a solution that is readily available. Unallocated resources, for example, are a kind of solution looking for a problem. A manager might easily define a problem so that the quick and easy solution is to throw some uncommitted money at it. Even when managers see that the problem is complex, they may feel that none of the alternative solutions carry a high risk of failure, that the cost of a poor decision will be low, or that a bad decision can be reversed later.

These ways of defining problems lead most often to quick action. Other ways of looking at and defining problems can lean to more complex, convoluted action.

Convoluted action is likely to result from a problem that is defined as having great importance to the organization "in terms of actions taken, the resources committed, or the precedents set."[3] Because of their importance,

MANAGERS ARE APT TO DISAGREE ABOUT THE DEFINITION
OF THE PROBLEM, ITS DIMENSIONS,   ITS IMPORTANCE,
AND THE CONTEXT IN WHICH IT IS EMBEDDED.

such strategically defined problems complicate the decision process. Such problems are not likely to have ready-made solutions waiting for them. Solutions must be developed, which takes time and adds to the complexity of the process. Such strategic problems also involve uncertainty and risk. Uncertainty means that more people will become involved in the decision as the manager reaches out to his or her network for advice and information. Uncertainty also increases the number of criteria that are applied to the evaluation of alternative solutions, while risk increases the amount of analysis put into understanding the problem. "There is more screening of projects 'that would bankrupt the organization.' "[4]

## The People Who Get Involved

Another contextual factor that operates powerfully in determining what type of action a problem will get is the involvement of people in the decision process. For the purpose of discussion, this can be divided into the effect of the *number* of people involved and the effect of the *types* of people involved.

A basic fact about decision processes is that the more people who participate, the longer it takes to make a decision and the harder it is to arrive at a decision. One review of research showed that larger juries (twelve rather than six members) take more time to deliberate and end with hung juries more often.[5] This same effect is clearly evident in any organization. As the number of people who will be affected by a decision increases, the more points of view there are to consider, the more need there is to make a decision defensible, and the more the process is likely to lengthen and grow complex. Finally, the more people there are who know and care about the decision, the more likely it is that they will want to become involved and so discover how the decision will affect them. Therefore, the more people there are who work on a problem, are affected by it, and know about it, the more complex and lengthy the decision process is likely to be.

The types of people who become involved in a decision also affect the length and complexity of the process. When the people involved are homogeneous, that is, when they belong to the same group, or work in the same function or at the same level, they are more likely to agree. Uncertainty about their preferences and needs is reduced, and the process can be commensurately speedy and simple. When, on the other hand, the people involved are diverse, when they work in different groups and functions and come from different levels in the organization, they are more likely to bring varied perspectives and agendas to the process. This complicates and lengthens the process even as it enriches it. Carter found numerous "influence tiers" at work in elaborate decision processes,[6] and Shumway et al. traced how a decision was transfigured as it worked its way up through several levels of an organization.[7]

In general, the more people and the more different kinds of people there are involved in a problem, the more time, communication, persuasion, and negotiation will be needed to reach a decision.[8]

## The Balance of Power and Vested Interests

The involvement of people in a decision affects the length and complexity of the process, but the relative power and the vested interests of those people modify their effect, sometimes making the process more complex, sometimes simplifying it.

The effect of power on the decision process depends largely on where the power resides. If one individual has the complete authority to decide, quick and direct action is likely. The decision of such a person can be made and implemented cleanly, without overt opposition. Hitler was an extreme example of this. As Albert Speer wrote, "Without much fuss, and without any rebellion on the part of those concerned, Hitler continued to make all the decisions himself."[9] The opposite effect is likely when power is diffused or when the locus of choice is different from the locus of authorization. Then, opposing interests must be reconciled, if at all, through accommodation, negotiation, and bargaining, which, as we have seen, lengthen and complicate the decision process.

In much the same way, the absence of strong conflicting interests will allow a swift and direct process, while their presence creates the need to resolve differences and win acceptance for the decision. This illustrates a point already made concerning the visibility of a decision. As a decision becomes more visible, it will attract larger and larger numbers of people with vested interests. To the extent that those people are powerful, their tendency to complicate the process further will increase. We would predict that a highly visible problem in which many important people stand to gain or lose would become a particularly complex and lengthy affair.

This brings us to an important point about decision making. Etzioni defined it well for us: "Societal decision making is not merely a thought process that balances goals and means, but also a political process that balances various power sectors." He went on to say that "knowledge can be ignored, power cannot." He also drew a distinction between the power to decide and the power to implement, which is akin to the distinction between the locus of choice and the locus of authorization.[10] Dubin also

THE BALANCE OF POWER

pointed to the effect of politics on decision making, especially as it concerns the amount of time needed to reach a decision: "The greater the need to accommodate differences . . ., the more time may be consumed in reaching the decision."[11] This fits with the finding of Mintzberg et al. that the eight decisions they studied which were characterized by intense political activity took an average of 3.6 years, whereas the less political decisions averaged only 1.6 years.[12]

These then are the major contextual factors affecting the type of action—from simple and direct to complex and lengthy—that a problem is likely to receive. As we have seen, these factors, all being a part of the same context, are deeply interrelated. How a manager defines a problem will influence the number and type of people who become involved, which will in turn influence the emergence of powerful others with vested interests of all kinds. Strategic, visible problems involving many people from different functions and levels will inevitably tend toward complexity in the decision-making process, while absolute urgency and absolute power can override these other more political concerns, thereby simplifying and shortening the process.

Having discussed the contextual factors that affect action, we shall now turn to the matter of the action itself. What does quick, direct action look like? What good can it do? What harm? What are the characteristics of convoluted, lengthy action? What are its advantages and disadvantages?

## ACTION: QUICK OR CONVOLUTED

No matter what type of action is required, effective managers appear to have a solid foundation from which to spring. Major building blocks in this foundation, some of which have been discussed earlier, include the following:

1. a compendium of technical, business, and political knowledge, based on intimate firsthand experience;
2. reliable sources of information, usually cultivated painstakingly and personally, spanning a broad spectrum of relevant areas (subordinates, customers, suppliers, etc.);
3. access to key sounding boards—people with whom a manager can "test the water" with minimal personal risk before jumping in; and
4. a reasonable, clear agenda, in Kotter's sense, which guides a manager in setting priorities and assessing the implications of action.[13]

Also important to managers is the willingness to act and accept risk. As we talked to managers, it was clear that the more effective ones were (a) willing to take hold of problems—in other words, to take responsibility for them, and (b) willing to "trust their gut"—to act on incomplete data on the basis of their experience and on intuition, even though they were bound to be wrong at times.[14] Such characteristics are often generalized as traits, such as aggressiveness, risk taking, need for achievement, and so on, but such generalizations mask the decidedly managerial quality of these elements—they are based on *specific business experience*. The traits alone, without experience, are insufficient and maybe even dangerous. This is why new managers (for example, fresh MBAs) and managers "brought in from the outside" often fail; they simply do not have the business knowledge and personal contacts they need.[15]

With this foundation for action in mind, let's first look at quick action, then at convoluted action: In each instance we shall first concentrate on the characteristics and utility of each type of action—the "theory" of that type. We shall then take a look at how managers see and use quick and convoluted action—the "practice" of each type.

### Quick Action in Theory

In general, quick action has three characteristics:

1. *Speed*. Managers deal not only in action but in fast action. Juggling so many things at once, with more coming at them all the time, they try to dispatch items quickly. "The ability to influence someone quickly can be enormously important to managers, who are often pressed for time."[16] They are constantly striving to get the proverbial monkeys off their backs. A problem is a kind of disequilibrium, a pressure, and managers "adapt to the pressure by developing alternatives that will lead to its rapid dissolution."[17]

The theme of acting quickly emerges repeatedly in research on managers. Kotter, for example, describes as a key challenge for general managers "being able to identify problems ('fires') that are out of control and to solve them quickly."[18] Peters and Waterman describe excellent companies as having a "bias for action"—a results-first approach.[19] Sayles and Chandler describe the "heart of the matter" as "quickness of response," pointing out that the ". . . penalty for waiting is that in a good many situations corrective action is possible only during a brief 'window.' "[20]

2. *One decision maker*. Quick action by definition involves one person pulling the trigger. The manager may get input about the target in question and may also check out the decision to fire with some key players; but generally speaking, quick action requires a unilateral decision. This may mean that the manager in question has the formal authority to make the decision or that the manager is assuming authority until there is evidence to the contrary. The bottom line, however, is that the quick-action manager is clearly responsible for the action and, should questions be raised, is the one who has to defend it.

3. *Limited search for information and alternatives*. Managers often

truncate information search and analysis. Pressed into action, they can't afford the luxury of thorough investigation. Under pressure, decision makers use only a few salient dimensions to decide[21] and examine fewer alternatives.[22] Managers use other shortcuts, such as accepting the first alternative that meets minimal standards and settling for short-run solutions.[23] A practical example of short-circuiting decision making is the capital allocation process in organizations. Managers passing on proposals from below often assess the sponsor of the alternative (including the sponsor's track record), rather than the alternative itself.[24]

Quick-action decision processes for disposing of complex problems are a fact of managerial life. Normative decision-making theories may disparage shortcuts to decision closure, but these theories also appear to be out of touch with significant portions of organizational reality. "The organization usually begins with little understanding of the decision situation it faces,"[25] so action can promote fuller understanding. Managers fend off the barrage of demands raining down on them by resorting to expeditious methods for understanding and acting on problems. A manager will try the hip shot if it seems that the problem might go away that way and if he or she can get away with it (that is, has enough power, few people involved, and little enough opposition). Quick action often serves managers and organizations well.

Among the advantages of quick action, compared with a strategy based on comprehensive analyses of the problem, are (a) action-first strategies do not demand a deep prior understanding of the problem; (b) they make much lighter cognitive demands on the decision maker; (c) they give visible evidence that attention is being given to the problem; and (d) they serve notice to other potentially interested parties that the problem is being addressed and can allow those parties to get in on the action.[26]

Quick action, however, can spell disaster. Some snap decisions ought to be more carefully considered. Sometimes corners cut in searching for relevant information turn out to be the heart of the matter. A prime example is the failure of decision makers to know intimately the situation they are deciding about.

Snap decisions also get made when taking alternative action is inconceivable.[27] An example is commitment to negative courses of action. Because of a strong emotional attachment to a previously adopted course of action and the political need to defend against criticism of it, administrators often respond to failure by recommitting themselves to the decision. Instead of reconsidering the decision, the administrator decides, almost without deciding, to persevere. "When an administrator is worried about keeping his job or fending off critics within an organization, he is . . . likely to increase rather than decrease his commitment to a previously chosen policy and . . . to become inflexible in his defense of such positions."[28]

Quick action can also be undone by the social homogeneity that makes consensus easier to reach. Just as homogeneity reduces one course of uncertainty by making the behavior of one's associates more predictable, it reduces dissenting opinions that can prevent mistaken decisions. Bennis states this dilemma as it applies to the manager and his or her subordinates:

> The enormous overload burdening every top leader makes it impossible for him to verify all his own information, analyze all his own problems, or always decide who should or should not have his ear or time. Because they are so important to him, he wants key assistants of kindred minds and compatible personalities. This means inevitably that the leader is likely to see only that highly selective information or those carefully screened people his assistants decide he should see.[29]

Thus, social similarity streamlines the decision-making process but also greases the skids.

## Quick Action in Practice

The managerial foundation for quick action is built from the same elements underlying the discovery of problems (see Chapter 2): digging and direct experience. Because of active, ongoing information gathering and accumulated experience, problems requiring quick action are seldom total surprises. While they may be unexpected (in the sense that the timing of the event was unpredictable) or even unlikely (you don't lose a major customer every day), there are almost always clues that a crisis is in the making or at least an expectation that "these things will happen." A case in point was one executive's description of an unpredicted, serious cost overrun on a project during a period of rampant inflation. The executive's own reaction:

> I was surprised, not that it isn't perfectly normal these days. Most everyone has a cost overrun on nearly everything they do. Of course the manager is responsible for it: either directly responsible or . . . responsible for having people that goofed up. Sometimes it just can't be helped. I mean with inflation going as it has been for the last few years, you can allow for it, but you seldom can allow enough.

And the executive's expectation for the reaction of the board of directors:

> . . . they nearly all have had the same thing happen to them at one time or another. For the most part, unless it's a completely stupid thing that should have been avoided 100 percent, they'll just scowl at you. . . .

So the first major element in understanding quick action problems is a managerial set that the unexpected is to be expected, that it won't be the first time it ever happened, and, short of clear incompetence on the manager's part, it won't be the end of the world. Further, because it or something like it has usually happened before, the manager is not operating in the dark—few quick-action problems are completely novel in all respects.

This kind of managerial set is highlighted by a crisis or catastrophe. Studies of these situations show that organizations that handle them well have prepared for them in advance. They have accepted that a crisis can happen and have tried to develop ways to detect the early signals. In addition, they have developed prevention and preparation mechanisms to put into effect when early warning signals are detected and limitation and recovery mechanisms to use if the crisis cannot be averted.[30] In other words, the unexpected is expected, and quick action is not a panic reaction.

A second major element is that managers can get information quickly if they know their people well enough and if they have an operational network of contacts:

> Growing up in this company, I've worked with all these people. I know them. They know me. You can't overestimate the importance of interpersonal relationships—they help enormously when you need something quickly.

Managers consistently described making an initial and very quick assessment of the situation through conversations with a few key players. A corollary to this is checking out the tentative decision with a few "reliable" people before acting on it:

> There are maybe two people's opinions you value more than a hundred people's.

This process includes figuring out how central people will react by "passing it by them" or by asking trusted people how these others are likely to react. Even under intense time pressure ("it was going to cost a lot of money and I didn't have time to run it by everybody"), effective managers invariably test the water before plunging in on an important matter.

At first, this might sound like glib advice, given that previous experience can blind a person to other alternatives and that the two or three "reliable sources" might be too similar to the manager. As we dug deeper, we saw that managers take some precautions against these pitfalls. These quick-action strategies include (a) dissection of the problem, (b) credibility assessment of sources, (c) direct involvement in the problem; and (d) consideration of personal proclivities.

First, quick action does not imply accepting the problem as given or that an immediate, total response is necessary. Most of the managers we talked to immediately questioned "emergencies":

> Why today? What's going to happen between today and tomorrow that will make a difference? Why is it an emergency? Why do we have to decide now? What makes it important?

These questions usually revealed that only a part of the problem was really urgent—that limited immediate action would buy the time for more information search and analysis:

> I think you'll find that only a portion of the decision is really urgent. You can make just that portion go ahead a little *and* have time to gather data before you commit to the whole thing.

In a compressed action sequence, a few more hours or days can make a substantial difference.

In addition to decomposing the problem, managers also quickly assess the risks involved:

> How bad is the wrong decision? What happens if we're wrong? You have to consider what your losses could be, and if they're tolerable, you can go ahead. Of these alternative disasters, pick one.

Considerations in assessment of consequences include whether a decision now will leverage future action that the manager wants (a way to move toward a larger agenda—see Chapter 3); whether it sets a precedent or course of action that can't be changed later; whether an available action can solve the problem at all, even temporarily; and whether the decision can be implemented quickly enough to matter.

A classic case of a situation requiring quick action is the business turnaround. Research on new general managers in turnarounds reveals that the effective ones dislike making quick, suboptimal decision but realize that even a crude tourniquet beats bleeding to death.[31] They were, however, judicious in their choices about where to apply tourniquets (as noted above) and "when new managers and their subordinates had fewer problems to deal with . . . they would go back and improve the tourniquet systems and processes they had installed earlier."[32]

Second, reliance on a few sources does not necessarily imply that they are "yes men." Managers consistently described assessing the credibility of the sources they used, placing heavy emphasis on their personal knowledge of the people and the degree to which opinions and advice from divergent sources correlated. Their focus was on "who can shed light on the problem," not solely on "who are my friends." In some cases managers deliberately sought out devil's advocates, particularly in assessing worst-case scenarios.

A third mechanism for guarding against pitfalls is direct involvement in the problem. Descriptions of quick-action decisions carry a heavy component of drop-everything-else-and-get-in-there-yourself. Managers typically talk to their sources directly, delegating critical activities only to their most reliable people. It's not unusual for the manager to go to the site of the problem "to get a firsthand look at the situation." The responsibility for a significant quick decision seems to increase distrust of secondhand information and assessments.

A fourth precaution taken by many managers is a quick inward look:

> There's always an emotional component to these things. You have to check the problem against your emotional hot buttons, your own personal biases.

Many of these managers were suggesting that if the emotional surge is too strong, you need to slow down and look again. A major reason for this is that a quick-action decision is likely to be wrong or at least need modification later. The stronger the personal commitment, the less likely a manager can be flexible later when it may be necessary to alter direction. Further, highly charged emotional reactions may lead a manager not to tap certain other people, whose input to the situation might be critical.

### Rules for Quick Action

Boiled down to a few "rules," the experience of managers facing quick decisions might look like this:

1. Build a foundation for quick action by (a) knowing as much about the business as possible, and (b) cultivating reliable sources of information and advice.
2. Quickly acquire information about the problem from a few reliable sources.
3. Decompose the problem. Act immediately only on the absolutely urgent part and buy time for the rest.
4. Test the water before acting, even if only with a few key stakeholders.
5. Control your exposure by choosing alternatives that leave room for maneuvering later, when more information will be available.
6. Close the loop. Figure out how the situation arose in the first place and what could be done to make it better the next time.
7. Don't shirk your responsibility. If you need to act, act, even if information is incomplete or there are risks involved.
8. At the same time, don't let yourself be set up. Don't assume that "crises"—especially those brought to you by other people—are always what they seem.

### Convoluted Action in Theory

If quick action is at one end of the decision continuum, then convoluted action is at the other end. Convoluted action is not compact; it is fragmented, extended, iterative, interrupted, and delayed—it takes one step backward for every two steps forward. It is a diffuse decision-making process which Connolly characterized as (a) involving several people from different organizational levels, units, and/or geographic locations; (b) containing several distinct activities; and (c) requiring considerable time between initiation of activity and "the" decision.[33]

Decisions about strategy are instances of convoluted processes, unless of course a team or top executive takes matters into his (or her) own hands and changes strategy or adopts a new one unilaterally. A top-down approach should be the exception, not the rule, since it is generally a mistake for strategy to "happen way up there, far removed from the details of running an organization on a daily basis."[34] This was Hayes's point too in his critique of ends-ways-means methods of strategy formulation. He argued that the process should be reversed, with strategy growing out of an organization's means—that is, its employees' capabilities. When strategy is defined from the bottom up or emerges in a means-driven way from the organization's experience, the process is convoluted. Strategic process is likewise convoluted when it is understood as including not just a strategy's definition but also its implementation.[35]

Mintzberg et al.'s model of strategic decision making (see Figure 4-1) is one representation of the convoluted action sequence. It contains a so-called main line plus all kinds of loops off of it. One loop is diagnosis: Once the decision maker has identified a problem tentatively, it must be clarified and defined further. As Mintzberg et al. state, "No strategic decision situation comes to the decision maker preformulated."[36] Another major loop off of the main decision-making line is development. Development, the heart of the strategic decision-making process, consists of (a)

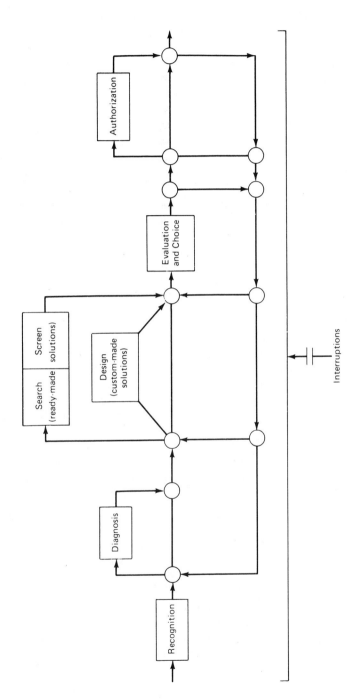

**Figure 4-1  A Model of Convoluted Action.** Adapted from Mintzberg et al., 1976.

search for solutions and (b) in lieu of given or ready-made solutions, the design of custom-made ones. "The designers may begin with a vague image of some ideal solutions. . . . The designers grope along, building their solution brick by brick without really knowing what it will look like until it is completed."[37] As these authors point out, development is often a nested activity, containing numerous repetitions of the same cycle. For example, one or more cycles to find a ready-made solution may be followed by a series of design cycles to modify it. Recycling is represented in the model by arrows extending downward from the main line and back to an earlier point in the process.[38]

Another loop off the main line is the authorization cycle. Those who develop and choose among solutions are often not those who authorize or approve the chosen courses of action. Authorization can also recycle as it proceeds from one level to another in the organizational hierarchy.

In general, convoluted action is dynamic and erratic, not a steady, undisturbed progression. It is filled with interruptions, delays, and regression as well as progression. Mintzberg et al., for example, found an average of 2.4 major interruptions in their study of 25 strategic decision processes.[39]

Convoluted action contains various degress of thickness. A relatively slim version is a strategic decision for which a ready-made solution or the modification of an available solution is adopted. A more elaborate version results when a solution must be designed from scratch. At yet another level of analysis, one can talk about strategy as patterns in decision streams.[40] Beyond a certain point, the layers of thickness inherent either in the complexity of the problem or in the thorniness of the social-political situation pile up until the problem defies solution altogether; it becomes intractable.

Convoluted action, then, has three characteristics:

1. *Relatively long.* Convoluted action takes a long time, often months or even years. It is not an orderly process by which closure is reached in a single meeting or a short series of meetings. Dubin has argued that the "time scale of decision is very much (and I want to underscore the 'very much') longer than the formalistic analysis of decision making would lead one to expect."[41]

2. *Multiple parties involved.* Unlike compact quick action, convoluted action is diffuse and fragmented. Many people get involved, multiple interest groups stake claims on the decision outcomes, and the progress is interrupted, delayed, and waylaid as it wends its way around unexpected turns toward completion. As Sayles and Chandler describe it, this kind of "decision making is a process in which various organizational levels and interest groups compete for a position in a sequence and to make their voice the strongest."[42]

3. *Extensive search.* The various subcycles of convoluted action—formulation of the problem, extensive search for solutions, long-term de-

velopment of an original solution, authorization loops—generate large amounts of information bearing on the technical and political aspects of the problem.

Convoluted action makes it all but impossible to take matters into one's own hands. The sheer magnitude of the problem requires that a broad spectrum of specialties be represented. The strategic significance of the problem means that numerous segments of the organization want to get their oars into the decision process. Because of the size and complexity of the problem, it is investigated thoroughly. If no preexisting solution meets the organization's needs, a long-term process is undertaken to develop an original solution. For all these reasons, a decision-making process of this type gets convoluted and becomes long and drawn out.

But convoluted action can be advantageous. It is consistent with the manager's organizational situation: Because they are woven into a complex web of interdependent relationships, managers must take account of these manifold interested others. There is no escaping the need to persuade, bargain with, or at least neutralize these other forces that would influence the outcome of important organizational decisions. In addition, convoluted action is politically sound. Rather than act now and fight it out later, as managers given to quick action do, managers engaging in convoluted action touch political bases and fight battles as the decision process moves along. However tortuous, convolution has the advantage of bringing to bear the different resources needed to crack complex organizational problems.

Convoluted action also has its drawbacks. Politics can take over, the struggle for organizational advantage supplanting the struggle to solve the problem. Taken to an extreme, this tendency can bring a slow-moving process to a grinding halt. Then the thick cycle becomes totally intractable. Another disadvantage is that what is workable politically may not be the best solution. Compromise is not always the best solution even if it sells better. Finally, convoluted action can take so long to produce a decision that by the time it comes through the political spanking machine it is obsolete.

## Convoluted Action in Practice

As we talked with managers about the kinds of action produced by different problems, we found that the same classes of problems could produce either quick or convoluted action. Some routine issues require convoluted procedures or just get out of hand; quick fixes, especially after the first flurry of quick decisions, can evolve into tangled issues; requests from subordinates for authorization may begin long sequences of events. The primary differentiating factors were a *relative* lack of urgency and the appearance of conflict among (internal or external) vested interests. But most of the problems resulting in convoluted action were specific opportunities tinged with a strategic component: opening up a new mar-

CONVOLUTED DECISIONS ARE THOROUGH.

ket, entering a joint venture, developing a new product, or starting up a new business. Also typically convoluted were decisions about general strategic direction: phasing out businesses, reorganization, allocation of resources. In general, as the stakeholders a manager has to deal with are located increasingly laterally, upward, and externally, action takes on increasingly ponderous dimensions. A graphic example of the extreme was provided by Murray, who described the attempt of a major electric utility to build a nuclear power plant. The decision was made by the utility in April 1970, but a year later these plans were blocked and the construction permit was withheld by the Atomic Energy Commission.

Because of the delay, the utility made alternative plans to supply energy; they decided to add a fossil-fuel facility to meet near-term demands. But this plan, too, was halted—this time by the U.S. Corps of Engineers, which was concerned about environmental impact. Later, the U.S. Fish and Wildlife Service jumped in and accounted for further delay. Although the decision to build this fossil-fuel facility was made in 1972, the final construction permit was not obtained until 1976. Note that Murray takes up the study of the decision-making process after the internal phases have been completed and deals only with the organization's attempt to implement a decision in the face of opposition from the outside. If the additional time taken to make the decision internally were included, the decision-making process would be that much more lengthy.[43]

A second example came from an interview with an administrator who led the convoluted effort to build a parking garage for a large university. The effort began in the mid-sixties and was completed in 1982. Under pressure from the university, which desperately needed the facility, this manager had to resolve major issues with (a) the neighborhood, which actively resisted university expansion; (b) the city, which has a love/hate relationship with the university; (c) strong factions within the university, each of which had its own ideas about what should be done; and (d) the state government, which had to rule on both zoning and financing for the project.

Whether the problem was as extreme as these two examples or just highly complicated, managerial descriptions of convoluted action contained four core elements: There was a "champion" who knew the "critical core" of the desired solution; numerous strategies for handling conflict were used; controllable elements were controlled; and personal contacts were used to advantage (and cultivated where necessary). The total process was characterized by improvisation, fluidity, and "strategic" intervention. Whereas quick action conjures up a wild-west image of a heroic figure, convoluted action suggests a shepherd, gently nudging a flock in more or less the same direction and taking an occasional shot at a wolf.

### A Champion

The major danger of quick action is a hasty decision that commits the organization to the wrong course. With convoluted action, the major danger is that the decision process will go down altogether, leaving a major problem unresolved. Thus, the absolutely critical aspect of convoluted action is that someone is committed to getting the problem solved and stays with it throughout the extended, winding, and often tortuous road to resolution. The tenacity—almost fanaticism—of the managers who shepherded these processes reminded us of Peters and Waterman's description of "product champions"—people who are so committed to what they are doing that they overcome all obstacles.[44] Champions of convoluted decision processes have this personal commitment and take on problems that they consider important. Sometimes they even fill a vacuum, latching onto a problem that falls in a never-never land of responsibility. But more than just accepting responsibility, champions stick with it, even as layer upon layer of complexity emerge (the sheer magnitude of convolution can seldom be predicted in advance). Loss of a champion is almost inevitably the death knell of convoluted action because pulling the linking pin allows all the factions to float off. As we will see, strategies for shepherding involve so much groundwork and personal initiative that a champion is not easily replaced.

By definition, convoluted action involves conflicting interests. There will be trade-offs, so the champion must know how much can be given up en route to a larger end:

> You've got to ask yourself, "I want to do a certain thing. Am I willing to give up some of this other stuff that maybe isn't as pertinent in order to get the end result?" And the answer, most of the time, is "Absolutely."

Managers are forced to compromise by virtue of their location between higher management and their direct reports. When the boss has a stake in an issue, it's folly to ignore it. But how do managers know where to give and where to draw the line? We're back to the same primary theme: You know because you know your business inside and out. You know the critical core, and you know the people and how they think.

We suggest, then, that effective convoluted action depends on a specific champion who (a) has a deep, emotional commitment to the issue, (b) is extremely knowledgeable about the business, product, or service in a

direct, hands-on way, and (c) is willing and able to stay with the problem long enough to work it through. In convoluted processes that had died, executives had almost always violated the champion principle. The problem may have been turned over to a committee or task force, it may have been assigned to a person without personal investment, it may have been given to an analyst or staffer with no firsthand experience, or the original champion may have been promoted or transferred in mid-process.

### Strategies for Handling Conflict

Managers in the midst of convoluted action constantly talk about negotiation—usually with multiple parties, many of which oppose one or more aspects of the proposed solution. We were struck first by the managers' acceptance of the political component of action, not as a necessary evil, but as a fact of life—a challenge to be met. By not placing a negative value judgment on the political process, these managers were able to approach the negotiation in a problem-focused, calculating way, going *with* the reality rather than spending time and energy trying to change it. As it turns out, the bargaining aspects of convoluted action are behaviorally specific, and, although there are few universal rules, there was consistency across managers in certain tactics:

1. Keep the various parties separated or at least only loosely connected. As Sayles and Chandler put it after observing project managers negotiate the shoals of vested interest:

> The manager seeks to avoid being confronted with a solid bloc of opinion or pressure by keeping the parties with whom he must deal *partially* fractionated.[45]

A basic principle of negotiation is finding the common ground between you and each of the parties, while avoiding having the other parties find their common ground against you. The manager seeks to preserve whatever room there may be for give-and-take and informal negotiation with *each* party, and that means dealing with each on its own ground.

2. Work with people, not abstractions. The world of managers is people—knowing whom to trust, where their "hot buttons" are. In the midst of convolution, managers seek to avoid dealing with abstractions, entities, or departments.

The complexity becomes comprehensible in part because the pieces come to be represented by people with whom there are relationships.

Because of their large networks and experience, managers may already know many of the parties involved. When they don't *they take the time to build a relationship.* As described by these managers, key features of this process involve establishing credibility ("I ignored some requests from my boss's office to earn credibility with the city."); respect ("I proved they'd cheated us and made them pay us the money. Why did I do that if I wanted to marry them? To get some respect. I'm not a pushover."); an image of honesty ("I was sensitive about my history and didn't try to disassociate myself from it."); and basic integrity ("If you exploit the other party, you always lose.")

3. Follow the basic rules of negotiation: Find a way for everyone to win. This was best put by an executive describing an elaborate negotiation to set up a joint venture with a competitor:

> Where are our needs and their needs? We're each different—how can we do something that is a win-win that satisfies his need and mine at the same time? You look for natural synergy. You have to benefit both parties in any negotiation—I don't care whether it's a union or customers. If you don't benefit both parties, it's a lost situation. Sooner or later, you're going to lose.

Far from a wishy-washy, insincere effort to make the other party like them, or a macho "don't cross me" stance, these managers talked about balancing opposites:

> They've got to understand I'm a tough son-of-a-bitch. I'm going to get what I want, but I am a nice guy. It's sort of a romance stage, like you go through with a girlfriend. It isn't all romance, but you learn to live together.

4. Really understand where people are coming from. There is a tendency to believe we understand someone else's perspective because we can imagine ourselves in that role. The managers we talked to emphasized that that is not enough. You have to understand the person in that role:

> You have to put yourself in his shoes. You say to yourself "if I was Mr. X and I had his personality. . . ." You have to understand his personality, not just his job. You have to realize that that's a person with needs and unique feelings and little neurotic qualities. That's a person who needs to feel comfortable with certain things. You learn about people by dealing with them and asking them questions. Listen to the things they talk about when they tell war stories. You learn about the person's insides by listening to how he gets his kicks—what really turns him on. If you can just get him to talk, just listen. Once you learn what makes him tick, then you can sell him.

In summary, handling conflict in convoluted decision processes requires that each party be treated on its own terms; which means face-to-face contact with an individual, understanding how that individual views the world, and negotiating for mutual gain from a basis of mutual respect. Much of the energy expended in convoluted action is directed toward establishing that kind of relationship with *each* of the critical interests around the problem.

## Controlling Controllable Elements

A great deal of the shepherding process involves image management. Often this is more of a problem with internal groups than with external—given a press to resolve a problem, the lengthy process may appear to have stalled. It is important for the champion to maintain the image of progress. Failure to do so may result in someone else taking over or the organization's abandoning the project. The other side of the coin is the danger of overplaying—by making overly optimistic promises or by involving other people in violation of "let sleeping dogs lie." Managers describe this precarious balancing act in terms of synchronized control of visibility and involvement. A major role of the champion is to decide when visibility or involvement are necessary and when staying low-key is important. Thus, few of the managers in convoluted processes talked of formal plans, major briefings of all parties, and the like, except as a short-term tactic. In general, the more visible the process, the more difficult it is to improvise, allow give-and-take on issues, use natural flows with various parties, and keep the elements separated. Formal deadlines, public stances, and hard criteria all served to reduce the champion's flexibility in dealing with the complexity. Managers tried to keep internal representation of the project highly selective, using allies, buffers, and advocates to protect their freedom of action while at the same time avoiding the appearance of a clandestine operation. This artistry was best described by one manager:

> An important part of this is to orchestrate. To get the drums going at the right times and pausing at the right times. It's getting people to see the musical potential, getting small groups to play the duet. You have to work behind the scenes, nudging people one at a time in the desired direction.

## Using Personal Contacts to Advantage

While the champion is obviously the key to convoluted action, he or she cannot act alone. Especially as the complexity of a problem increases, a manager's success increasingly depends on the ability to leverage other people's talent. Some of this comes with the job—the authority to call on staff resources, for example—but once again the key theme from the interviews was building personal relationships. In time, virtually all the managers we talked to had cultivated relationships by doing favors, helping out when others needed it, and generally avoiding making enemies ("You never know—the person you just stomped on may hold the keys to your next project."). When they needed help, they could call in the chips. Often all that was needed was a door-opening introduction, or a word to a major party that the manager could be trusted. Sometimes the need was for advice on how to handle a particular person or an opinion on strategy. In other cases, the manager needed someone else to "play the heavy" or

"take the flak." In short, the more convoluted the process, the more managers must draw on other people for help and the greater the variety of kinds of help needed. This kind of leverage cannot be created overnight or for each problem as it appears. It's something the individual manager must create over the course of a career.

## Rules for Convoluted Action

Just as there seem to be some "basic rules" for quick action, managerial experience with convoluted action seems to contain some consistent principles:

1. There must be a champion. The manager who takes charge of a convoluted decision process must be committed to resolution of the problem and willing to tackle the ponderous bulk of the political process.
2. The manager must know the critical core. Because trade-off and compromise are inevitable, the manager must know enough about "the business" to know when a concession is crippling and when it doesn't matter.
3. The manager needs to be an adept negotiator. Various parties involved need to be treated individually, personally, and with mutual benefit in mind.
4. The manager should know that struggle is a way of life with a long-term convoluted decision process, especially if its objective is to innovate. The manager must be persistent, or as the president of a fast-

growing, high-tech company told one of the authors: "The only way to succeed as an executive is to grind it out."

5. The manager has to control tempo and images. Through artful manipulation or visibility and involvement, the manager can keep the process moving forward (show progress) without losing flexibility (the inevitable consequence of public commitments).

6. The manager should use personal leverage. Managing convolution, while dependent on an individual, is not an individual act.

7. Above all, it is necessary for a manager to be patient. The foundations for convoluted action around a specific problem take time to build—and many of the elements can't be short-circuited. It takes constant action on many fronts to bring it all together in the end.

Although at opposite extremes of the decision-making continuum, quick and convoluted decisional action are very much interrelated in organizational life. A manager may, for example, take a hip shot at a problem and discover that the problem is still very much alive and kicking—and even bigger than suspected. If quick action fails, it may educate the manager as to the true dimensions of the problem. In this way, quickness may lead to convolution, as a series of pokes gradually expands the problem domain. By the same token, convoluted action is not always a huge monolith but can be reduced to component parts, many of which can be solved quickly. For example, the decision to explore or abandon a single proposed alternative may be a snap decision. The convoluted process is, in actuality, a "plurality of subdecisions," and it is in this sense that one can structure or impart structure to unstructured, elaborate decision processes.[46]

## IMPLICATIONS FOR MANAGERIAL EFFECTIVENESS

On any given day, a manager is in the midst of many things. There are likely to be a number of quick-action problems underway and a few convoluted processes at various stages of progress. Effectiveness, then, cannot be gauged solely on a problem-by-problem basis but rather must be seen as a balancing act. It's not just how well a manager handles problem X, but how well he or she handles problems X, Y, Z, and N, all of which demand attention at the same time.[47] Part of that, of course, is whether X, Y, Z, and N are the "right" problems, but there is much more to it. Managers may have less choice over which problems they face than over the ways they act on them. As Kotter suggested in his study of general managers, the crucial test is the choice of actions that accomplish multiple goals at once. Does the quick action on problem X move forward a piece of Y? Or does it make solving problem Z must that much more difficult?[48] And this, it seems to us, is the remarkable quality of effective managers. Their apparently unrelated actions on widely diverse problems are, however erratically and spasmodically, moving them forward toward some larger goal. They love solving problems, but a problem is seldom an end itself. They seek consistency, but they don't hesitate to change direction. They love to win—but wars, not battles. In short, effective managers have a vision for the business that makes sense of unrelated problems and actions. This characteristic, a vision that is enacted through day-to-day action on even mundane issues, is one of the characteristics of excellent corporations.[49]

Once one realizes that managerial action is not unilateral use of power—that much of what a manager contends with involves people and problems that can't be controlled by brute force—then the insight by Sayles and Chandler takes on profound meaning:

> The effective manager widens or narrows limits, adds or subtracts weights where trade-offs are to be made, speeds up or slows down actions, increases the emphasis on some activities and decreases the emphasis on others.[50]

It is a guiding, nudging, orchestrating job requiring bold, quick action mingled with subtle and convoluted processes. Effective management requires both ends of the continuum: the ability to act on limited information and instinct to isolate and contain *and* the ability to shepherd convoluted political processes to a satisfactory conclusion. Further, effective managers can control their bent for action and results. At times they may encourage a convoluted action sequence because it will kill an idea or project. At times they may procrastinate deliberately, knowing that if they manage not to meddle, an issue will take care of itself.

Most managers are quick to acknowledge that they win some and lose some over time. What seems to differentiate those managers who win more than they lose is, in the most global sense, their ability to learn from experience. More than just the accumulation of knowledge and contacts that accrue to all of us with age, effective managers seem to view action as learning.[51] Whereas some people learn best through reflection and study, these managers create experience by doing things, quite often things they don't know how to do.[52] It seems a classic case of remembering the past yet being free of it, of viewing each new problem as a challenge to be tackled by action rather than through analysis and rumination.

The next chapter will examine these issues in more depth, but the point for now is this: Problems have no existence except through the managers who act on them. Earlier, we quoted an executive who pointed out that it's not enough to know another person's job—you have to know the job through the person in it. It's the same principle here: The manager acting on a problem is making that problem something unique. By the same token, each problem faced, each action taken, shapes what that manager will be. (See Figure 4-2 for a summary of this chapter.)

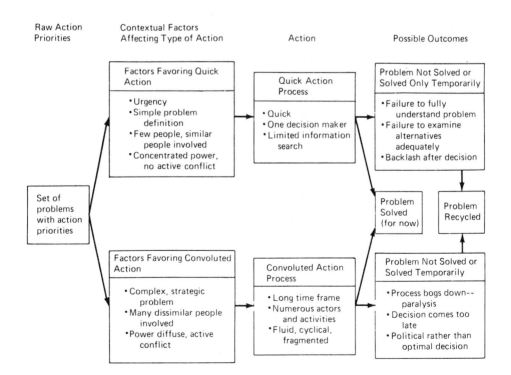

Figure 4-2    **Moving from Priorities to Action**

# 5

# *VICTORY*

# *OR DEFEAT*

Just who exercised the crucial influence in getting the jet program through was not too clear at the time, and it is certainly no clearer now when nobody wants to be singled out for fathering a failure.[1]

Mistakes are the very base of human thought, embedded there, feeding the structure like root nodules. If we were not provided with the knack of being wrong, we could never get anything useful done. We think our way along by choosing between right and wrong alternatives, and the wrong choices have to be made as frequently as the right ones. We get along in life this way. We are built to make mistakes, coded for error.[2]

## AFTER ACTION, THEN WHAT?

Managerial decision making is a complex process involving streams of information and events that get recognized as problems, a complex set of factors that affect what problems will get attention, and still another set of factors influencing where the continuum from quick to convoluted the action will fall. Once action is taken, everyone watches attentively to see what will happen. Routine actions with foregone conclusions are ho-hum affairs, but bold strokes fascinate people. The players and interested spectators look on like hunters watching to see whether a rifle shot has felled a deer. This kind of drama surrounded the press conference held by the Johnson and Johnson CEO after poisoned Tylenol killed several people in the Chicago area. How would he handle this extremely delicate moment with a shocked nation looking on?

Managers take action not for its own sake but to achieve results. Was the problem solved, the opportunity exploited? The consequences flowing from decisions are diverse, whether the decision is a discrete, quick action or a convoluted accumulation of actions that adds up to a completed project or an enacted policy.

The decision may be no decision at all but a failed attempt to decide. One manager we interviewed evoked an almost existential despair and complained poignantly about management's inability to act:

> Management team meetings are frustrating to me because we discuss things but we come out with no solutions, recommendations, nothing—just smoke.[3]

Or if a decision is actually reached, it is not necessarily implemented. Another manager from the same organization lamented the fact that problems which management supposedly solved remained unresolved because responsibility wasn't clearly determined:

> There are cases where a problem comes up and it's dealt with, but too many come up and either we don't arrive at a solution or it isn't clear who's responsible and it comes up again and again. . . . We're horrendous on follow-up.[4]

Or if the solution is implemented, it may not work, and the manager is back to the drawing board—assuming the manager doesn't become discouraged by the setback and avoids the temptation to rationalize the failure. Or a decision can be made and action can actually follow, but the result may not be what was intended. As one executive told us:

> Sometimes you make a decision, and what you get is exactly opposite from what you anticipated. A beautiful illustration is the Germans bombing London [during World War II]. They thought they would destroy the morale and they got exactly the opposite.

Even if the action has the intended effect, it may also have unintended consequences. A corporation we are acquainted with has launched Quality-of-Worklife projects in its plants, projects with sufficient bite that workers have responded by becoming much more involved in the corporation's renewed effort to produce quality products. But as production workers have taken more responsibility and become less alienated, their foremen and supervisors have unexpectedly lost motivation. In beginning to solve the problem of work alienation by expanding their responsibilities, management has inadvertently alienated first- and second-level supervision by, in effect, shrinking their jobs.

Finally, solutions that work and produce no special negative side effects don't endure forever. Managers solve a problem and, if the solution sticks, they turn their attention to the host of other problems clamoring for their attention. But the solution doesn't necessarily last, not because it wasn't a good solution, but because times change. A human resources executive told us a story:

> A number of years ago I convinced my superiors that we needed to do something internally to accelerate the whole process of developing high-potential managers. So we created a management course, an off-campus course for managers who were on the upbeat in the organization. . . . That course was extremely popular and because it was so popular, we tended to memorialize that success and we didn't change it. We didn't modify it as we should have over the years. Finally that decision caught up with us and the company.

So having emerged victorious, managers can't afford to become complacent because solutions wear out and eventually need to be repaired or replaced.

Another kind of problem that pops up in the wake of success is one that has remained in the background while a more pressing situation has taken precedence. One of the authors acted as a consultant to a plant with severe employee relations problems, which after several years of work were alleviated. No sooner did this vertical, labor-management problem recede than a horizontal, interdepartmental problem arose to take its place. The rivalry among departments had been there all along, but the managers, having only limited attention and energy, couldn't attend to it until the crisis in labor-management relations had abated.

Actions and consequences are often thought of in terms of decision and implementation, as seen in the following comment by a general manager:

> Making decisions is easy, but getting them implemented sometimes is nearly impossible.[5]

Although it is common parlance to talk of decision and implementation, we prefer to see implementation as, in many cases, itself consisting of a "plurality of subdecisions,"[6] each of which has to be implemented. It is easy to overblow the importance of the decision that authorizes a capital expenditure, an acquisition, or a divestiture, and to underrate the work that follows as mere implementation. A corporate executive argued this point:

> Winning the battle for approval for the main action should not be confused with developing the strategy for how the battle lines will be drawn and how the battle will be fought. The action plan to follow is likely multi-phasic and requires no less careful thought than the main action itself. If somebody, having received approval of an action, just goes ahead and acts without thinking through the various steps, they're likely to stub their toes.

In managerial life, then, there is no rest for the weary. Problems flowing to the managers may get disposed of permanently, but they are just as likely to take up residence. If managers get approval for a solution, then they may next have to implement the solution or oversee the people assigned to implement it. When they try to implement a decision, the solution may fail and put them back on square one. Or the solution may work but in the process create a new set of problems that gets dropped in the manager's lap. Nor can managers expect a problem to stay solved, because solutions unravel as the problems they were designed to solve evolve over time. There is no end to problems, even for effective managers:

> A vice-president who seemed to have the whole thing under control confided in me one day that he felt he was in a small sailboat going through the storms at sea. He would work furiously to get the boat out of one storm, only to have one or even two or more descend on it at once. There was no breather; it was constant crises. . . .
>
> There were times when there were storms within storms, whirlpools, and sea monsters all at once. "The phone will ring and I'll think, 'Please don't let it be another problem. Please let it be a solution to one that is here now.' "[7]

Given this complexity, it is no surprise that the consequences of managerial action are not always clear victories or defeats. The world of the manager is rarely amenable to simple, unambiguous learning. Kanter has even suggested that managers operate under an "inverse law of certainty": "The more important the management decision, the less precise the tools to deal with it . . . and the longer it will take before anyone knows it was right."[8] As one manager we interviewed put it:

> In management there are few clear victories. There are so many gray areas. That interminable gray is what causes stress. The things that stay constantly unresolved are the ones that sap your strength.

While bankruptcy or a million dollar cost overrun appear to be concrete indicators of the quality of managerial decisions, the causes of such

outcomes are usually quite complicated. Seldom are such things caused by a single managerial decision, nor is it obvious that a different decision would have changed the outcome.

The first thing to recognize, then, is that the consequences of managerial decisions are ambiguous and can be interpreted in different ways. In some cases it is not clear what action was taken. Other times the action is clear but the consequences are obscured. In still other cases, action and consequences are obscured. In still other cases, action and consequences may be clear, but the relationship between the two may be murky.

## THE AMBIGUITY OF ACTION AND CONSEQUENCES

People have always wanted causes that are simple to comprehend, and about which the individual can *do* something.[9]

Just as the original recognition and definition of a problem involves the interpretation of ambiguous information and events, discovering the consequences of one's action is often a matter of interpretation. The first hitch is that the *action itself* may be seen differently by different people. Managerial decisions, particularly important ones, usually comprise a set of smaller decisions made over time. Not all participants is a decision cycle may agree that a decision has been made of what it was. A tabled project, for example, may be viewed as postponed by one manager and terminated by another. (Helping to shroud action is the tendency of some managers to sidestep clear responsibility for decisions.) As a university administrator explained it:

> People here don't like to make clear decisions because they're held account-
> able. They prefer to talk around things, and then act on them. If it works,
> fine. It not, then heads don't have to roll.

The second hitch is that the *consequences* of action, like the action itself, are subject to different interpretations by various participants. This is particularly true for tough problems where effects may take a long time (months or even years) to appear. Was it the new president's aggressive marketing stance or the improved economy that increased sales last year?

Decision making cannot be divorced from a manager's values.[10] Managers place different emphasis on outcomes such as return to shareholders, quality of work, and social responsibility. Shareholder returns may be measured as market share by one manager, profitability by another, and may be viewed in either the short run or the long run. Because decisions have multiple consequences, the criteria used to evaluate a decision will depend on which consequences are emphasized by whom. The development of a technological marvel that is ahead of its time may be a success to the R&D manager but a failure to the sales manager hunting for a market.

A case in point is IBM's STRETCH computer, a machine of advanced design developed originally for atomic research in the late fifties. For technical and marketing reasons, the program ended up losing $20 million. Thomas Watson, Jr., pronounced the computer a disaster, an assessment that certain technical people and certain high-level executives did not agree with. In fact, when it later became apparent that the innovative STRETCH technology influenced the design of subsequent, successful computers, even Watson changed his mind about the computer.[11] History gets rewritten with the passage of time. Years later, Watson said about the costs of developing the computer: "A better fifty million we never spent, but it took seven or eight years to find out."[12]

In another sense, too, consequences are hard to pin down. When managers choose a course of action, they pass up other alternatives and can never know what would have happened if they had taken another course. One executive made the point this way:

> I walked down this road and I don't know where that road would have gone
> because this is the road I chose. So you never really know whether that was
> the right decision to make. For example, I was responsible for equalizing the
> vacation between exempt employees and hourly and non-exempt employees.
> I argued that if vacation is a time of rest and recharge, then the non-exempt

and hourly need that time as much as the exempt. It did wonders for the morale of the non-exempt, and the exempt felt that we had taken something away from them. So we changed the vacation policy, and the change worked. But the paths we looked at and didn't choose may have worked better or worse. There's no way of knowing.

Managers never know what would have happened if they had chosen what Robert Frost called "the road not taken."

A third hitch is that even when actions and consequences are known, the *connection between* them can still be ambiguous.[13] This is because there is usually a time lag, often a long one, between an action and its results. It has been estimated, for example, that ". . . it takes three to five years of blood, sweat, and tears to get a company 'turned around again' after a crisis."[14] One executive stated:

> I guess there are relatively few actions taken where the structure is so simple that the action is taken now and the consequences follow immediately. That isn't in the realm of management. If I punch the key on the typewriter, the consequence is that the letter is imprinted instantaneously. And so the consequence follows immediately after the action. But in the typical management process, an action or series of actions are taken and then in the period following are the consequences. And there are other variables so it's not just my action which affects the consequences.

During a lag, then, many things can happen other than implementation of decision, and knowing what actually "caused" the result can become problematic. Ilgen, Fisher, and Taylor provide an interesting example, noting that there are primitive tribes which are unaware of the connection between intercourse and childbearing. The reason for this is the nine-month delay between conception and birth, during which time other events occur, most of them extraneous to pregnancy.[15] Similarly, organizational decisions have consequences which may be uninterpretable even well into the future.

An additional consequence of the lag between decisions and results is that the people who have to live with the results may not be the same people who made the decisions. To the extent that turnover in management is rapid (20 to 40 percent per year, according to some estimates) and lags are long, decision makers leave results behind them for the next incumbent. This has been a particular bane for U.S. presidents who face the results of their predecessors' programs. The general public tends to blame the incumbent for failure to solve problems that resulted from the decisions of others.

Conversely, managers sometimes get credit for good performance that they were not solely responsible for. They may have succeeded, for example, with the help of excellent staff support. This tendency to credit a person and overlook the person's circumstances has been called the "fundamental attribution error": We tend "to underestimate the impact of situational determinants and to overestimate the importance of personal factors."[16] But behavior is shaped by situation as well as personality. This tendency causes problems when a manager's effective performance is assumed to reside in his or her person and to be transferable anywhere. Functional managers are promoted to general management positions, and general managers are transferred from one business to an entirely different business, and they sometimes fail because of this.[17] Thus, because the connection between action and consequence is misread, managers are moved beyond their sphere of competence and the Peter Principle strikes again.

The connection between actions and consequences can also be muddied by the weak correspondence between the magnitude of decisions and the magnitude of their consequences. March and Olsen note that "tiny (and essentially unpredictable) variations in events can make large differences in final outcomes."[18] The "minor" decision by party functionaries to raid the opposition party's headquarters may escalate to full-scale impeachment proceedings and resignation of the president of the United States, as happened with Watergate. The converse can also happen. Major organizational interventions sometimes have little real impact on the organization or its performance.[19]

In summary, a variety of forces act to blur the interpretation of

WHY DO I GET THE FEELING THAT THE PETER PRINCIPLE IS ABOUT TO STRIKE AGAIN...

action, consequences, and the relationship between the two, particularly for convoluted decisions. Determining what happened is more a matter of negotiation and impression management than an objective assessment of facts.

Meetings held to examine a decision may produce a variety of interpretations of the consequences. Those who have supported a decision tend to judge it a success, as did the executive quoted above about the decision he had made to equalize the vacation benefits of exempt and nonexempt:

> You have to live with yourself—you're pretty good at rationalizing that what you did was the right action. In fact, today I still think it was the right action. I don't feel it, I know it. I don't have any data to say it was the right action; all that comes internally.

Decision makers stick by their guns, even in the face of overwhelming evidence opposing their position. Napoleon provided a pure case of this in his disastrous Russian campaign in 1812, when he proclaimed:

> In affairs of state one must never retreat, never retrace one's steps, never admit an error—that brings disrepute. When one make a mistake, one must stick to it. That makes it right![20]

Decision makers may even manipulate and distort data on the decision's effects in order to support their case.[21] The control over interpretation systems is a powerful means to shape the evaluation of outcomes.[22] The annual stockholders' report and the company newsletter contain excellent examples of how even the most noxious events can be presented in a positive light through selective emphasis on certain aspects rather than others.

## CONSEQUENCES, WHILE AMBIGUOUS, DO MATTER

> I do the very best I know how. . . . If the end brings me out all right, what is said against me won't amount to anything. If the end brings me out wrong, ten angels swearing I was right would make no difference.[23]

Consequences, like problems, are what people make of them. One person's example of poor management is another's example of overwhelming environmental forces that no one could predict. This fundamental ambiguity hardly means that decisions do not have consequences. It is the *importance* of the *interpretations* of consequences that in fact causes such investment in figuring out what happened. (This is particularly true when there is a hint of failure; managers are much more sanguine about success.)

There are at least three types of consequences of decisions: First are the effects of decisions on the formation of precedent, both for the organization and the individual manager; second are the impacts on relationships resulting from participation in or exclusion from the decision cycle; and third, decision-making success or failure becomes a manager's track record.

Decisions accumulate. Problems tend to recur. These two elements mean that, in time, satisfactory decisions set precedents for the policy, rules, and procedures guiding future action. In short, the organization moves toward making the handling of problems routine. Strategic direction is often the result of a series of decisions made over time, each of which influences the succeeding decision.

An analogous process goes in in the manager's head, as accumulated actions become cause-effect models of the world and how it works (see Chapter 2). This is probably what is meant by experience or organizational savvy.

It would be inefficient for either organizations or managers not to routinize decision making. No one would ever have time to solve problems if every problem required a novel response. Newspapers, for example, have evolved structures and procedures to routinize the handling of unexpected, fast-breaking news events.[24] These attempts to establish efficient action sequences for problems are, however, a mixed blessing. The development of formal procedures, rules, and policies affects all aspects of the decision cycle, from problem recognition to the type of solution chosen. The very efficiency of such guidelines creates a subtle pressure to define new problems as old problems, to choose priorities without thought, and to use historical solutions rather than generate novel ones. This is particularly true when managers respond to crises; then tend to rely on proven programs, concentrate on improving efficiency, and avoid innovative solutions.[25]

Thus, the making of decisions creates consequences through the evolution of precedent (often formalized into procedures) and through the accumulation of decisions into strategic directions. But the decision-making process also affects relationships among the people involved. People whose advice is taken seriously are likely to have positive feelings. Those who were not involved and feel they should have been, or whose advice was solicited but ignored, are not likely to feel so good about it.

The nature of the interactions between the central decision maker and his or her peers (or others over whom the manager has no formal authority) lays the groundwork for future cooperation. In convoluted decision making, many such people may be involved, and responsiveness to their concerns will affect their willingness to involve, or be involved with, the manager in future problem solving. Specifically, convoluted decision processes require a manager to consider carefully whom to involve, the degree of involvement, the timing of involvement, and whom to inform of the outcome. If there is conflict among the people involved, the manager has the additional diplomatic task of dealing with the people who "lose out."

As mentioned in Chapter 4, quick decisions also affect relationships, largely with those people who feel they should have been consulted. In this case, the manager must devote energy to unruffling feathers or run the risk of alienating people who may be important in a future situation.

Relationships with superiors are also affected, especially when a decision must be "sold up" to higher management. Exposure to managers at levels higher than one's boss is usually infrequent, so the impressions made can have lasting effects.

All of this is related to the track record of the manager. Put simply, a manager viewed as competent is more likely to get proposals approved than one seen as less competent.[26] A reputation for competence is formed, at least partially, on the basis of how often a manager is "right". So decisions, and particularly the perceived consequences of decisions, accumulate to separate the less successful from the more successful managers. It has even been suggested, for example, that managers seen as successful by the organization are those who dissociate from failure and associate themselves with success.[27] Researchers who have explored what distinguishes brilliant "risk takers" from "foolish gamblers" have concluded that

> risky choices that turn out badly are seen, after the fact, to have been mistakes. The warning signs that were ignored seem clearer than they were; the courses that were followed seem unambiguously misguided. History not only sorts decision makers into winners and losers but also interprets those differences as reflecting differences in judgment and ability.[28]

Unfortunately, it is not always possible to dissociate oneself from failure. Failure is always an unwelcome guest in organizations, and if one manager adeptly avoids a given instance, it has a way of showing up on another manager's doorstep. When the Nixon administration's policy of supporting West Pakistan during the Indian-Pakistan war of 1971 became unpopular, President Nixon saw fit to disown the policy. In the public eye, it then became Secretary of State Kissinger's policy. "Nixon could not resist the temptation of letting me twist slowly, slowly in the wind."[29] It was weeks, too, before Nixon stopped avoiding Kissinger personally.

Failure is a hot potato. Still, it is too extreme to say that if a manager makes a serious mistake, he or she is through. ("Good people are a scarce commodity, you don't throw away good people—unless it's a be-

IT IS NOT ALWAYS POSSIBLE TO DISSOCIATE

ONESELF FROM FAILURE...

trayal of trust or breaking the law.") But failure sets even good people back. Look what happened to the two individuals chiefly responsible for the development of IBM's STRETCH computer, judged at the time to be a disaster:

> At the time the program was killed, both the chief designer, Stephen Dunwell, and the executive in charge of it, Charlie de Carlo, had gone into the penalty box. Watson, recalling this, said "poor Dunwell had to crawl into a cocoon for three or four years, but I apologized publicly to him later."[30]

So it is understandable why managers put distance between themselves and failure; it hurts their reputations. The issue isn't likely to be settled by a single event, though how one handles failure can go a long way toward explaining who succeeds or derails in the executive ranks.[31] Rather, careers last a long time, and an action-oriented manager will have many opportunities to make decisions. Failing to take action can be as damning as making mistakes, and perhaps the ultimate wisdom in the matter came from a senior vice-president who said, "You have to be a risk taker, but you have to win more than you lose."[32]

## LIVING WITH THE RESULTS

This section, summarized in Figure 5-1, has several important implications. First, the consequences of important, complex decisions are essentially ambiguous. Like defining what a problem is, defining the results of

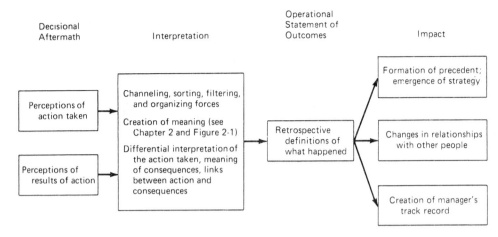

**Figure 5-1    The Ambiguity of Knowing What Happened**

action is an interpretive process. This means that it is subject to all the tendencies discussed earlier: People seek to reduce uncertainty, use simple models to interpret what's happening around them, and sometimes don't hear information contrary to what they are expecting. One way managers cope with ambiguity is to look for numbers, such as return on investment or percent of quota, as a means of being more objective. Forecasts, for example, tend to become the criteria against which to judge the efficacy of action. Similarly, many organizations have also invested heavily in management information systems that routinely deliver large amounts of quantitative performance data.

While all of these approaches can help in assessing decisions, they can also be deceptive. There is no magic in quantification, and, as was the case in recognizing problems, an overreliance on numbers can divert attention from the rich complexity of the issues. Numbers and trends are particularly risky in fast-changing environments where what has been true historically may not be true now. For instance, what was true for the oil companies when prices were controlled is not necessarily true under decontrol. What was historically unprofitable may not remain so, given world oil prices, depletion of supply, and inflation.

Given that consequences require interpretation even when numbers are available, what does this mean for managerial decision makers? First, they should be aware that *all* models of how the world works are simplifications of reality and that different people may use different models to explain the same events. In a sense, the rules that guide managers in assessing decision quality are figments of their experience.

Second, perceptions of consequences *are* taken seriously. They can become policy; they do become part of the track record of the manager

involved. On important problems, then, managers are well advised to negotiate perceptions of consequences—to try to reach some agreement with
important people on how it went. This process may work differently for the
quick decision cycles than it does for the convoluted. Effective quick-cycle,
action-first decision making depends on feedback. Knowing how a hip shot
turned out allows a manager to take corrective action, but the very efficiency of the quick cycle disinclines managers to spend time on follow-up.

In convoluted decision making, involving many people over time,
analysis of consequences begins during the decision process. The negotiation over what is important begins early in the problem-solving process;
involving the right people at the right times can create shared responsibility and common preceptions. On the other hand, involving numerous
people in diffuse processes may result in many of them never knowing
how things came out or what difference their contribution made.

Put succinctly, a manager needs to consider carefully what role to
take in negotiating the outcomes of action. A few "rules of thumb" can be
summarized as follows:

1. *Recognize that evaluating decisions involves management of perceptions.* For most day-to-day problems, what others think may be irrele-
vant. But for certain important problems, what others *think* happened
may be more important than what actually happened.

This means that managers need to consider both tactics and strategy
when problem solving. Knowing whom to involve, when to involve them,
and how to involve them is an intuitive but critical choice. In some cases
it is important to keep the decision-making process visible, especially
when the manager wants others to know that all reasonable efforts were
made. In other cases, the manager may want to keep a low profile, staying
some distance away from the problem and getting his or her act together
before letting the problem become visible.

What's important is the manager's awareness that decision making
is as much the management of a process as it is the making of a choice.
Assuming responsibility for a problem also implies responsibility for *how*
the problem is solved.

2. *Pick causes carefully.* This applies not just because it serves a
manager's self-interest, but also because solving problems is a question of
priorities and available time. Association with certain decisions determines one's track record. For this reason one executive advised:

> You have to know enough about your place in the organization that you
> don't take on the impossible task. Even if the idea is a good one, it may be an
> idea ahead of its time, or it may be beyond your scope in the organization.[33]

The other side of the coin is that convoluted decisions (which often result
from even trivial problems) consume time and energy. While managers

should not shy away from sticky problems, they should be realistic about investing effort in either the trivial or the intractable.

3. *Inoculate against risk.* Making decisions is a risky business, but so is avoiding decisions:

> Unhappily, corporate difficulties are more often the result of inaction in the face of a dangerous change than of being the hopeless victim of circumstances. It's the exceptional executive who can bring himself to admit that a crisis is in the making; the unexpected report of trouble, like Banquo's ghost, just doesn't fit into the scheme of things. Even fewer are the executives with the courage to take drastic action *in time.* On the contrary, case histories reveal too many instances where top management procrastinated about an emergent crisis.[34]

When assessing a problem, a manager should consider the consequences of failure to act as well as those of a potential action. At the same time, when contemplating a risk-filled decision, a manager should take certain precautions. To make this point, one executive recounted an experience in which he neglected to lay the groundwork for a risky decision:

> Probably the most unpopular decision I ever made was one made in collaboration with the then chief operating officer of our company. Our decision was to hold the line on wages in major collective bargaining during a year in which everyone else wasn't holding the line. We made this decision because if we didn't hold the line, we would no longer be competitive in world markets. I believed then, as I believe now, that the position that we took was the correct position. Ultimately, however, the union stonewalled our decision as finally did the board of directors of our company.
>
> In retrospect, the mistake we made was in failing to think through the consequences of the bold stand we were about to take. . . . Our decision was on the side of the angels, even though other companies didn't see the light. But because of the high-risk factor and the high-pressure environment, we should have, to a much greater extent than we did, exposed others to the several [possible] consequences of the action about to be taken. Had we done so, the end result—the immediate collective bargaining result—would have been the same, but the effect on us as chief operating officer and chief bargainer for the company would have been more favorable.
>
> Decisions that turn sour don't necessarily reflect unfavorably on the decision makers if they have involved the proper people in the process and they have carefully examined the consequences of the action to be taken. Bosses don't like to be surprised and surprise is what makes bad decisions unpopular and damaging to the individual decision maker.

The message is clear: Before making a risk-laden decision, managers must (a) anticipate as well as possible the likely consequences, especially the negative ones; and (b) touch base with at least some of the powerful people in the organization. Another executive echoed this advice when he told us how he went about deciding whether to take on a big project:

> I'd put the thing together the best I could and spell out in considerable detail what all the costs would be and what the potential payout would be—spell it out as well as I could. Then I'd take it to a couple of the directors [members of the board] that were particularly interested. Sit down and go over it. I knew that if these two guys went along with me, they had a lot of influence with the rest of the directors and chances are, if we all decided it was the right thing to do, there wouldn't be any drastic repercussions [if it didn't work out].

To protect themselves against downside risk, astute managers imagine the worst and line up allies who agree that the risk is work taking.

4. *Develop and use strong feedback systems.* Be aggressive in finding out about consequences. Experience is only a good teacher when the data one generates through action are collected and interpreted:

> The burned hand teaches best. After that, advice about fire goes to the heart.[35]

It is hard enough to know accurately the consequences of our actions, even if we have a good network; it is virtually impossible if we have no reliable information.

Since managers are reluctant to show themselves (or their superiors) in a bad light, news about failed solutions can be extremely hard to come by. A corollary to the inverse law of uncertainty mentioned earlier in this chapter is the inverse law of feedback: The higher a manager's position in the organization, the more constricted are the feedback channels upward. This law operates with a vengeance when, as one executive put it, "executives are susceptible to a belief in their own infallibility." One sure way to court disaster is to "persistently ignore early warning signals" or "even go so far as to block them deliberately."[36]

5. *Accept failure (your own), if it happens.* Even the best managers make mistakes: To be human is to be fallible. A successful head of a small company, talking about making quick decisions, asserted:

> EXECUTIVE:     I've made a lot of bad ones, I can tell you.
> INTERVIEWER:     But you made some good ones, didn't you?
> EXECUTIVE:     I made some good ones. I got lucky a few times.

Because executives so jealously guard their reputations as capable people, they may go to the extreme of never admitting mistakes. One executive said:

There are some executive suites and corporate environments in which the executive, if he makes mistakes (which, of course, every executive does) never lets those mistakes be seen by others. That's a self-destruct course. An executive who does that becomes uptight and withdrawn from his environment and out of touch with reality.[37]

In contrast, the effective managers we interviewed took a different tack. One executive said, "If things work out well, then I thank everybody. . . . If things didn't work out, and I was the driving force, then it's my fault." Similarly, another executive told us:

Everybody knows you make mistakes, so why not admit it. I make it a point to admit the blunders. Once I admit it, I feel better about it. It doesn't bother me. It's really a painful thing to keep trying to not admit some things. You have to carry that around as a burden until you get it off your chest.

In addition to admitting mistakes, it is important not to be defeated by them. An executive stated:

You just have to have the ego strength to lose and not let it discourage you. Every time you lose, you learn something. Every time you lose, it's another bit or piece of information that's going to help you win next time.

In not allowing oneself to be defeated, it is important to avoid the pitfall of staying with an initiative beyond the point of diminishing returns. Managers, especially the innovative ones, accomplish nothing unless they fight through temporary setbacks. Distinguishing between a losing proposition and a good cause gone bad is tough because "the time between an optimistic, can-do attitude and overcommitment is very thin and often difficult to distinguish."[38]

Defeat teaches, if the manager is willing to learn. But the temptation is strong to shun responsibility and to withdraw from the problem. One executive related cases in which production managers tried unsuccessfully to force a policy on the work force, and when the work force resisted, the managers gave up:

I have seen *other* managers who, faced with that kind of impasse, say "Well, there has to be a solution. We haven't found it but let's regroup. Why is it that the work force has resisted this?" And likely as not, those managers go to the workers and ask them why they're resisting.

A successful manager, a gutsy manager, is one who faces up to decisions that have failed and regroups and makes them less of a failure or sometimes even a success. In defeat, the effective managers neither fold their tents nor necessarily persist in the same course; they stick with the problem and consider *different* solutions. In one study, handling mistakes was one of five characteristics that distinguished senior executives who derailed from those who lived up to their full potential:

> Although neither group made many mistakes, the arrivers overwhelmingly handled them with poise and grace. Almost uniformly, they admitted the mistake, forwarned others so they wouldn't be blindsided by it, then set about analyzing and fixing it. Also important were two things the arrivers didn't do—they didn't blame others, and once they had handled the situation, they didn't dwell on it—they moved on to something else.
>
> Derailed executives tended to react to failure by going on the defensive, trying to keep it under wraps while they fixed it, or, once the problem was visible, blaming it on someone else.[39]

6. *Accept other people's failure.* It's no wonder, given the climate that prevails in many organizations, that people avoid failure like the plague:

> In my experience, if the corporation does something and it turns out well, then everybody had a part in the decisions. If it turns out poorly, then there's usually some guy that caused it.

Small wonder that so many managers are gun-shy about making decisions. An executive confided that he felt this squeeze in the last company he worked for:

> I ask myself, "why do I find decision making so easy now, whereas it was sometimes so difficult then?" The answer I came up with was, "Well, there was tremendous pressure from above to be right or else." There are some organizations that have little or no tolerance for people who make mistakes. Therefore people don't make mistakes.

They don't make mistakes because they play it safe. They avoid risks. Said another executive:

> The biggest problem with decision makers are the kind of guys who have to be right all the time. Those are the ones who are in deep trouble. They just have to be right every single time so therefore they're never going to take a risk.

To create a climate in which people don't have to be right every time and where they can feel free to take risks, managers can do a couple of things. First, they can encourage their people to try things on a small scale—modest experiments, which, if they fail, do no great damage.[40] Second, they can set a good example:

> You know, if you walk in and say, "God, did I blow that. Jesus Christ, did I screw up today" and tell a story about how badly you screwed up, they're

PEOPLE ARE USUALLY TURNED OFF BY BEHEADINGS.

going to be a lot more open to telling you things that they've screwed up. . . .
It works so well with the people at work, and they feel very comfortable in
saying to you when they've made a mistake. So you get more data, more
factual data, and they don't have to figure out all the rationalizations of why
what they did was right.

7. *Don't rest on your laurels.* When managers enjoy the sweet taste
of victory, they must be alert to the present dangers. For one thing, they
must remember to share the wealth. We have seen that it is easy to be
generous with blame; it is also tempting—but counterproductive—to be
stingy with praise. A university administrator advised:

> Much of what you do isn't personal; you don't do it by yourself. There are
> many actors. And the applause is great enough to share with everyone.

Echoed by several other managers, this advice is especially important to
managers who, like the one just quoted, expect to keep collaborators and
sponsors committed to a long-term project.[41]

The other present danger of winning is complacency. A certain mental inertia sets in and lulls the manager into extrapolating a comfortable
present into the indefinite future. As president of Pan Am, Juan Trippe
had become accustomed to an annual 15 percent market growth and
counted on that growth continuing when he made his company the
"launch customer" for the new wide-bodied planes:

> Talking about Trippe, the executive who was at the time Pan Am's chief of
> engineering said: "Trippe would not have looked at marketing analysis.

There was no planning department in Pan Am. Trippe sat in his corner office, made plans, and then made them come true."[42]

Unfortunately, as soon as the airline and aircraft industries became committed to wide-bodied planes, the early-seventies recession hit and the market for the planes evaporated.

Even with success, sustained success, managers must remain vigilant. Said one executive:

> When one's decisions turn out all right, one should resist the temptation to spend very much time basking in the glory of those right decisions. They need to be reexamined on a continuous basis to be sure that the decision that was right yesterday continues to be right today.

The manager must continually "sift through the good news looking for evidence of future problems."[43]

Unfortunately, handling victory is not the manager's greatest challenge, because most of what the manager does is contend with problems:

> Ninety percent of their time is spent on problems; ten percent on victory dinners, celebrations, etc. And very often the celebration for a wonderful victory coincides with the discovery of a terrible new problem. Rarely is victory unstained by a concurrent encroaching defeat.[44]

# 6

## *AWASH IN DECISION STREAMS: IMPLICATIONS FOR STAYING AFLOAT*

It is obvious from the preceding chapters that decision making in organizations is complex, often amorphous, and seldom amenable to simple prescriptions. Before trying to reach some conclusions about it, it may be wise to highlight some of the major themes we have covered.

The book began with several vivid examples of decisions, setting the stage for looking at decision making in terms of some basic parameters:

1. While there are discrete decision points, it makes more sense to look at streams of decisions. Decisions are really accumulations of sub-decisions, usually made over long periods of time.
2. Decision making is sometimes an individual event, but more often many people are involved in various ways and at various times. This is another reason to look at decision streams—problems as they flow through organizations—rather than at individual decision makers.
3. Decision processes do not unfold in logical, orderly stages. They double back on themselves, solutions are found before problems are understood, action on earlier problems affects current decisions, and so on. Because of this interwoven quality, problem solving and decision making are not separate activities.

4. Decision making by managers takes place in the midst of many other managerial activities. The fragmentation, interruptions, and juggling of managerial life have strong effects on decision-making activities.

Against this backdrop we looked at four elements of managerial decision processes: recognizing problems, selecting certain problems for action, taking action, and interpreting consequences. The word *elements* is carefully chosen; the four elements are usually present in any decision process but not as clear, separate stages or in any necessary order.

Recognizing and defining problems is an act of creation. From streams of events, information, and actions, meaning is created by managers through their own personal cogitations, or interactively with other people, or both. Problems are in fact what we make of them (or what someone else makes of them for us). The way pieces get put together to form a "problem" is affected by many forces, including a manager's stance toward information, the amount and types of information available, mental sets and perceptual filters, organizational structures and procedures, and power relationships among the players.

Selecting certain problems for action is of interest because managers are aware of, and confronted with, more problems than they can act on at one time. There are circumstances under which managers will deliberately choose inaction. Left to their own devices, managers prefer to work on nonroutine, current, and well-defined problems, frequently tackling them in sequential order. But the overriding reason that managers act on some problems rather than on others is the pressure to act resulting from a crisis, deadline, someone in authority, or some other source.

Action on problems can range from quick decisions (made by one person after limited information search) to convoluted decision processes (involving a diffuse set of actors and containing numerous subcycles). Which way action will go is influenced by many factors, including the way a problem is defined, the urgency of the situation, the availability of feasible solutions, the magnitude of the consequences, the people vested in the issue, and the political implications of including or excluding others. Working through a convoluted process or dealing with the aftermath of a quick action requires a hefty assortment of managerial skills, including negotiation, bargaining, using influence, diplomacy, and others.

Interpreting the consequences of action, like recognizing a problem, is a creative act. Action produces events and information, the implications of which are shrouded in ambiguity. The ways in which consequences are interpreted, however, have important implications: outcomes of decisions create precedent and result in strategic direction; they affect future working relationships and decision processes; and they affect the track records of the managers seen as responsible.

Where does this leave us? In an organizational context, managers are confronted with a stream of events, actions, and information from which they fashion meaning and take action (or vice versa). It is a fast-paced world of complexity in which judgment is a key resource and where fragmentation, negotiation, interruption, delay, and pressure are commonplace. The human limitations that managers bring into this setting—limited ability to process information, perceptual biases, reliance on simple models of reality, and the rest—are often blamed for the failures in decision making. In fact, these limitations are probably the only things that keep managers sane and make any action at all possible. A realistic view of managerial decision processes suggests that the search for the omniscient decision maker is not likely to turn one up. There are simply some things that no one can do much about. There are a few other things that individual managers *can* do something about. There are a few more things that organizations can tackle. But on the whole, the human decision maker in an organizational setting should hang on to modesty. Managerial decisions have been and will continue to be a product of judgment and luck as well as expertise. In such a case, slight improvement is no small accomplishment.

## THERE ARE SOME THINGS NO ONE CAN DO MUCH ABOUT

Solving important problems will never be the logical, orderly process that most of us strive for, no matter how orderly the plan. Defining problems will remain an evolutionary process affected by points of view, vested interests, and the bits and pieces of information available at any given time. Pressures will ebb and flow, shifting attention from one problem to another, changing definitions, involving and excluding various individuals. Sometimes the real problem won't materialize until well into the decision-making process or maybe not until after some action has been taken. People will take hip shots when they should have been more thoughtful; relatively simple problems will at times end up in tortuous and tortured processes. Finding truth will remain problematic.

There will be no peace for managers: The world won't stop and wait for a decision. The inherent complexity of many managerial problems is confounded by the nature of managerial work. Managers will continue trying to juggle many things at once, to deal with fragmentation of their activities, to retain vast quantities of oral information, to cope with flitting from topic to topic in brief episodes, and to deal effectively with the endless procession of individuals making demands on their time. The process of management is fluid, shifting, unpredictable, and pressured. The constant tension will remain between the press for action and the need for analysis.

Simply getting through the day for most managers puts a premium on proficient superficiality,[1] and this means that the decision-making process will seldom go unaffected by the swirl of managerial demands.

Managers can't escape human nature. As much as they may expect themselves and others to do the rational thing, people are not always reasonable. Emotions inevitably cloud thinking. Concern about oneself is often at war with larger concerns. No matter how bright managers are, they can't transcend the limits on their information-processing ability. Nor can they help bringing their biases, a product of their histories and present circumstances, to the task of interpreting information.

As irrepressible as human nature is the nature of human organization. Collections of people cannot come together without labor being divided, specialties forming, rivalries developing, a pecking order emerging and evolving. Authority is meted out by a formal hierarchy and grabbed by people eager to have it. Decision making, then, is always influenced by the competing interests and the power differentials among decision makers. Likewise, all present actions are shaped in part by the set of past actions; an organization's history shadows its decision makers:

> Executive leaders cannot undo history; they inherit situations in which predecessor leaders, rival leaders, cooperating leaders have created flow lines of decisions that circumscribe and envelop their own decision making.[2]

The organizational environment will not leave managers alone, nor will it easily succumb to their attempts to control it. The ball game can change dramatically and suddenly in midstream. The more the environment is characterized by fast change, the more likely that managers will be buffeted by quickly changing pressures for action (and the resulting hop from one problem to another), by compression of convoluted cycles due to time constraints (and possibly a higher percentage of either paralysis or applying tourniquets to convoluted problems), and by problems that are fuzzy and remain so past the point where action must be taken. Coping with fast-changing conditions is likely to force decision making lower down in the organizational hierarchy, where managers directly affected can take action quickly. This will result in greater decisional demands on lower-level managers. The overall impact is that largely uncontrollable forces will continuously upset the logical, orderly flow of decision streams.

Some aspects of the organizations in which managers are embedded influence decision processes but defy managerial control. A hospital's dual administrative and professional hierarchy, the control of schools by external boards of elected officials, and changes in federal regulation are all examples of structural givens that have direct effects on decision processes. Managers can learn to live with and work around such features, but they are unlikely to change them much.

Organizations also carry with them a host of "facts of life" largely determined by the products or services they exist to provide. Government regulation, for example, goes along with certain activities (like operating nuclear power plants), and managerial decision making must adjust to it as long as the organization continues to engage in those activities. Higher education provides another example: The number of undergraduates to be educated is directly related to the birthrate twenty years ago. In short, the types of problems "thrown forward" and the decisional processes that can be applied to them are constrained by the nature of the business one is in.

In summary, many of the convolutions of decision making, the hectic pace of managerial life, human nature, environmental events, and certain organizational characteristics are part and parcel of managerial decision making in organizations. For the most part, a manager can do little more than live with them. As Robert Heinlein once observed, "If a grasshopper tries to fight a lawnmower, one may admire his courage but not his judgment."[3]

To note that there are some givens is not to say that managers are powerless. Rather, it is to point out that sometimes the apparent helplessness of the decision makers around us is not always their fault. Further, when we occasionally fumble ourselves, it is not always a sign of personal ineptitude. If people do not always seem rational in their decision making, it may be that the circumstances they face are not entirely rational either.

## SOME THINGS INDIVIDUAL MANAGERS
## CAN DO SOMETHING ABOUT

The danger in emphasizing that there are things we can do little about is that instead of just providing solace it might provide an excuse to do nothing or to get sloppy. But managers are seldom totally helpless, even when decision making is heavily constrained by uncontrollable or barely controllable forces. It is a mistake to use chaos as a reason to throw up one's hands or to make decisions without thought on the assumption that it doesn't matter anyway.

Managers define risk in subjective ways, paying a lot of attention to the magnitude of possible bad outcomes (at the expense of considering the magnitude of possible benefits). Further, managers are prone to think of themselves as taking more risks than they actually do, and they learn less than they might from the outcomes of the risky decisions they do make.[4] This suggests that many managers may be overly conservative decision makers already, without the added incentive of thinking that matters are out of their hands.

Making random decisions, or making arbitrary decisions without thought, is self-defeating as well. Our message is that it is often impossible to use a rational, systematic decision process—not that it isn't desirable to do so. Managers should seek, whenever possible and as much as possible, to lay out alternatives, systematically evaluate them, and decide

on optimal strategies. Given that managers can't always do that, then, being able to make decisions in other ways is an additional crucial skill. To make the most of the latitude available to them, managers must (a) exercise the choices they do have, (b) know the organization and business they are in, (c) know themselves, and (d) develop and use a wide variety of skills.

First, exercising the choices managers do have is often subtle, involving, for example, deflections at certain key junctures in an unfolding decision process. It is often possible, for instance, to affect the definition of a problem by providing information or by taking charge in an ambiguous situation. Choice can also be as subtle as varying the timing of action—the decision to act now or later. Similarly, it can simply—but significantly—be a matter of attacking a problem while it is still fuzzy and hard to read versus holding off until it is unmistakable and full-blown. Managers also exercise choice when they decide how to respond to pressure—by determining, for example, whether the pressure is real or exaggerated by people wanting to force a given outcome. By buying time, managers find room to maneuver. They also find space when there doesn't appear to be any by declining to accept automatically other people's definitions of a problem; they may elect to unwrap a seemingly packaged problem before disposing of it. In a similar vein, they can find breathing room in apparently cramped quarters by, for instance, making the best of orders—by finding the good parts in a directive they generally oppose. In this sense, they *use* rather than surrender to realities.

So, much of the discretion available to the manager resides in the choice of which problems to work on, what battles to fight, and when to cut one's losses. In making these choices, proactive managers are guided by yet another area of discretion—the short- and long-run agendas they have set for themselves. It is here, we believe, that the importance of having a vision stands out. Even if the world of managerial action is murky, convoluted, contradictory, and capricious, managers who have a direction—a larger sense of purpose—are in a good position to take advantage of those qualities. It is that vision that makes it possible to see linkages among seemingly unrelated events, to see how day-to-day decisions can accumulate to larger ends, to take advantage of leverage, deflections, and vacuums. Without vision, managers can only react to events. With purpose, they can shape events and be on the lookout for efficiencies; they tend to choose courses of action that solve more than one problem at once.

To take effective advantage of these and other areas of choice, managers need to know the organization and business they work in. This knowledge is only modestly acquired by reading and hearing secondhand accounts; it comes primarily from firsthand experience. To learn in this way happens only over time, which is why managers who grow up in a business have a leg up on those who do not. Because it is very difficult to learn a business and organization inside and out, there are real limits on how "general" a general manager can be; that is, how widely applicable is his or her managerial expertise.[5]

No small part of knowing one's world is knowing the people who inhabit it. Beyond understanding them and knowing what to expect from them, the manager must, of course, form viable relationships with them. This is another reason why it is difficult to transfer into a new organization: The newcomer is bereft of the network of relationships indispensable to managerial effectiveness.

To exercise choice effectively, managers also need to know themselves. Do they have the manager's essential qualities—basic optimism, intelligence, ego strength, interpersonal skills (of several different sorts), knowledge of the business, comfort with ambiguity? Can they adroitly mix knowing and acting, always putting as sound a knowledge base as possible under each action they take and, at the same time, using each action as a chance to learn? Do they reflect moment to moment as they act? Are they in this sense exemplary reflective practitioners?[6] In what respects is their managerial makeup and repertoire wanting?

No manager comes, or even becomes, fully equipped, but the better ones recognize their deficiencies and adjust accordingly. If they know their limits, then they can choose to bring in help. If they know their hot buttons, then they try to make allowances when they overreact. As one executive told us: "It's important for the executive to know himself or herself, and to examine his or her inventory of skills, talents, interests, likes, dislikes, and then build a personal executive strategy around these skills and talents." To achieve and maintain a realistic view of themselves, managers with high aspirations must overcome the reflex reaction against evidence of their shortcomings or limitations; their need to *be* competent must outweigh their need to *appear* competent. This inner stance can be difficult to assume if the ambitious manager has, in fact, achieved an elevated position with its many signals of the manager's importance and value to the organization.[7] Most of all, successful managers must come to know and gain a modicum of control over the driving forces within them that determine so much of how they act and learn.[8]

Managers can create latitude and capitalize on it by developing and using a diverse set of skills. Effective managers know when to take quick, decisive action and how to deal with its aftermath. They are adept at shepherding long, drawn-out decision processes—the nudging, negotiating, coordinating laterally, selling upward, and rallying downward. They are skilled at digging for information; they listen, question, dissect, probe beneath the surface, consider the source, attend the cues as well as words, and resist the impulse to punish the bearer of bad tidings. They learn how to weigh the intangibles, grasp the ambiguous, and be comfortable with

MANAGERS HAVE TO BE GOOD AT BOTH
QUICK AND CONVOLUTED ACTION.

the unexpected. They are capable of trying new things and likewise of ending experiments that fail and cannot be fixed. No one has all the skills, but managers who make the most of their jobs have a basic appreciation of "how to create a process that makes things happen."[9] Especially as they rise to higher levels in their organizations, they recognize that their job is not so much to make decisions themselves as to manage the decision-making process.

An important part of making things happen is creating a management team to participate in decision-making. The characteristics of upper-level teams, not just the senior manager in charge, have been shown to influence organizational outcomes, including strategy formation and implementation.[10] So the name of the game is selecting the right individuals, helping those individuals to develop on the job and in the classroom, and fostering the right chemistry among team members, including the manager.

In summary, managers sometimes can control decision making directly, but they often have to settle for critical deflections. Key to this are an awareness of the complexity of decision processes and the availability of a broad range of skills that can be drawn on at the appropriate points. Awareness permits identification of key junctures in the decision process that can be influenced. The skills permit action, whether that action be negotiation, bargaining, manipulation of pressure, or whatever. The analogy of streams for describing the decision process is apt: The flow of water can be diverted by various methods applied at strategic points.

As a closing point, perhaps the most significant thing managers can do to improve their decision making is to improve their abilitiy to learn from experience. Where does one learn how to take "thoughtful action" (a term attributed to Karl Weick which captures making decisions with care, attention, reflection, and purpose)? An article by Isenberg suggests that "an essential element of skilled professional practice is a practitioner's ability to reflect on actions while performing them."[11] The ability to make effective decisions can be learned, but, like any other difficult skill, learning it requires considerable effort.[12] Managers must (1) be willing to make decisions or find situations that force them to, (2) be willing to accept the consequences of making mistakes and to dig out the learning that mistakes have to offer, (3) seek out and watch closely how good decision makers do it, and (4) constantly search for new situations that permit the development of different skills.

## SOME THINGS THE ORGANIZATION CAN DO SOMETHING ABOUT

Managers work in organizations, and no matter how effective individual managers may be, they are fighting an uphill battle if the organization does not support effective decision-making practices. Organizations affect the quality of managerial decision making in at least four ways: through the values and tone they transmit, through their structure and design, by the career and developmental opportunities they provide for their managers, and by the business strategies they enact.

Corporate values and the tone of decision making are rather broad and intangible qualities. As anyone who has ever worked in an organization knows, however, the intangible can be very real. It doesn't take long to figure out, for example, whether an organization's dominant value lies in solving problems or in adhering to the bureaucracy. Most employees "know" the extent to which an organization will support a manager who takes intelligent risks (and makes the inevitable mistakes that come with them).

Values, culture, tone—whatever one wants to call the atmosphere around decision making—are not conveyed by the proclamation and statements of corporate philosophy. They are set by the organization's actions. If managers who take a risk and fail or admit candidly to failure are punished for doing so, they will be less likely to do those things again. If short-term goals are emphasized or if competition among divisions or functions is fostered, then decision-making practices are not likely to reflect long-term thinking or cooperation across boundaries. This theme has been developed by Kerr who discussed at length the folly of rewarding one thing while hoping for another.[13] It is not enough to hope that managers will take risks, share information, cooperate fully, think long term, and so forth, if their organizations do not reward these activities.

As we have seen in earlier chapters, effective decision making often requires acting without all the information, and it demands using a broad array of contacts, the majority of which lie outside of hierarchical chains of command. In some organizations, both of these activities put a manager at high risk, particularly if the decision is wrong. To encourage the risk taking that is so critical to innovation and problem solving, the organization must transmit its values through actions that (a) encourage experimentation, (b) give managers lots of rope to try out different problem-solving strategies, (c) develop a reward system consistent with experimentation and risk taking, and (d) show tolerance for the sometimes "deviant" behavior that experiment-minded managers may show. How does an organization do this without creating chaos? Peters and Waterman suggest that excellent corporations manage it by selective use of loose-tight controls. They place tight controls on a very few, carefully selected values (for example, IBM's emphasis on service to the customer) and give a lot of freedom in other spheres.[14] The bottom line is simple: An organization cannot expect its managers to *be* effective decision makers if its culture prevents its managers from *behaving* as effective decision makers.

Thus, what initially appears as an intangible, even mystical, culture or set of values is, in reality, quite concrete. It materializes in the actual reactions of the corporation to managerial initiative in decision making. It is also manifested in the organization's structure and design. To deal effectively with an uncertain, fast-changing environment, for example, an organization may need to be decentralized, with the locus of decision making lower down and with fewer binding policies, rules, and formal procedures. In decisional terms, managers close to the action need the latitude to act in response to unfolding events. If an organization adheres to a rigid hierarchy and formal procedures in such an environment, decisional processes will likely suffer: Solutions won't be timely because problems may change before decisions can be made, information may not be used because the people who have it are not in the vertical line of command, and so on. Nor will strategy get shaped low enough in the organization by the people who possess the means by which the organization gains its competitive edge.[15]

An organization that wants its managers to take responsibility for decisions will reflect that desire by making structural and design decisions that facilitate managerial action. There is likely to be less emphasis on formal rules and authority, thereby allowing managers to bypass normal channels. Allocation of resources may be more flexible, permitting quicker response to opportunities and to experiments that work. Information systems may be designed to aid (rather than expose) the managers who need timely, succinct, and focused information. Staff functions may be created to serve the line, rather than to control, monitor, or annoy it.

Other manifestations of organizational commitment to effective managerial decision making appear in the career and skill-development opportunities available to managers. Recent research has confirmed that the vast majority of learning for managers occurs on the job.[16] It is through the types of assignments managers have that they can learn the critical lessons in decision making. Yet many organizations have no systematic way of identifying the key assignments for their managers, and then they compound the error by filling critical roles with managers who are "already proven" rather than with those who stand to develop new skills. As should be clear from our discussion so far, the many skills required for effective decision making are not "born in" nor do they develop through a single job or seminar. They are the product of a career with different kinds of challenges, enough latitude to take risks, and enough support to learn from mistakes. Such development requires an organizational commitment to its managers that encourages a career in the organization (the only real way to develop a knowledge of the business) and a willingness on the part of the organization to take as much risk (especially in assignments) as it expects its managers to take.

A final point is suggested by Peters and Waterman who point out that excellent corporations "stick to their knitting." That is, they focus their business strategy on what they know how to do, what they are good at.[17] As we have seen, decision-making effectiveness is highly dependent on managers' knowledge of the business and their networks of contacts. Business strategies that lead organizations to hop in and out of businesses, products, and markets can adversely affect the decision-making performance of managers. This is probably why Kotter found that general managers don't have skills with unlimited transferability; they depend on an intimate knowledge of the business and the people associated with it. Without these, a manager can rely only on more generic knowledge, for example financial analysis, which seriously limits the decision-making process.[18]

In summary, organizations probably have more control over decision streams (though maybe not over specific problems) than do individual managers. The tone that is set in terms of the behaviors emphasized and rewarded, the way the organization is structured, the developmental op-

portunities available, and the nature of the business strategy can have dramatic effects on decision processes and on the individual managers involved in them. Of course, this use of the word *organization* is loose— people make many of the decisions that create the systems and structure of an organization. Organizations are the legacy of a myriad of management decisions—Grand Canyons of decision streams, built over long periods of time. They are, by their nature, hard to change. But organizations can be changed, and it may be through their potential influence on the organization that members of top management can have their greatest impact on decision making.

## Searching for Direction

As Table 6-1 shows, there are many things endemic to the decision process in organizations that no one can do much about. On the other hand, individual managers can have impact on specific problems and various parts of the decision process, sometimes directly but often through subtle deflections. The organization can have substantial impact through its sys-

**TABLE 6-1   Some Apparent Realities of Decision Making in Complex Organizations**

| Some Things a Manager Cannot Expect to Do Much About | Some Things Individual Managers Can Do | Some Things The Organization Can Do |
|---|---|---|
| The fact that decision making in organizations is not a totally rational, orderly process | Exercise choices in the problems to work on, which battles to fight and where, and when to cut losses | Set values and tone to support problem solving and risk |
| The nature of managerial work: the juggling of problems and conflicting demands | Develop intimate knowledge of the business and good working relationships with the people in it | Design organizational structure, reward, and control systems to support action rather than bureaucracy |
| People are flawed: they are limited information processors, have biases and emotions, and develop vested interests | Know yourself: know your strengths, weaknesses, and hot buttons, and when to ask for help | Provide assignments where decision-making skills can be developed |
| Fundamental forces in the business environment | Develop the diverse set of skills necessary to act in different situations | Keep business strategy focused on things about which management is knowledgeable |
| Basic organizational components determined largely by the business one is in | | |

THE ORGANIZATION'S DECISION STREAMS ARE
BUILT OVER LONG PERIODS OF TIME.

tems and structure, but more of its influence affects decision streams rather than specific problems. So what?

First, research and training in decision making, as abundant as they are, have focused on the individual decision makers facing discrete problems. The prescriptions have been disheartening because they often directly contradict some realities (they ask managers to operate in areas they can do little about) and ignore others (the major impact of organizational values and structures). While managers fumble with their laminated cards that tell them when to involve subordinates or that outline the logical phases of problem solving, the subtle yet critical skills involved in deflecting and guiding complex decision processes are ignored, as are the skills required to act quickly under pressure.

Second, organizations (or more properly, their managements) bemoan the apparent cowardice of their managers, who don't pass on negative information, are afraid to take risks, don't have "the big picture," or are always covering the exposed portions of their anatomies. These concerns often translate into pressure on the staff to improve management selection and training. The reality may be that the organization is rewarding short-term performance and punishing risk—the new crop of carefully selected and trained managers will fare no better.

Third, managers sometimes fail to realize how many opportunities there really are to exert some sort of influence on decisions. Some abdicate entirely, blaming "the system." Others try to take full control, ignoring the roles that other people play in important decision processes (resulting many times in resentment, resistance, or sabotage).

Given the complexity of decision making in organizational settings, it is no surprise that these (and other) problems exist. Solutions, if they exist, are not obvious and will not emerge from an exclusive focus on either individuals or organizations. Neither will solutions emerge if the important but largely uncontrollable contextual factors of decision making are ignored. The need for additional research is clear, and it seems time to shift the focus of that research from individual cognition, small groups, and mathematical models to a more holistic, *in situ* look at the decision process. It is fortunate that existing research forms a strong foundation from which to tackle the larger complexity.

We offer the following three suggestions for the future study of managerial decision making:

1. Don't get tangled up in semantic arguments about differences between problem solving and decision making. In the managerial world, these activities are so entangled that distinctions among them are only of semantic interest. Focusing on one or the other excludes critical pieces of the decision process: choice is not, in reality, distinct from problem definition, the examination of potential solutions, and so forth.
2. Keep all the pieces in. To understand what managers face, it is critical to preserve the context of decisions. Central elements include dealing with more than one problem at a time, fragmented activity patterns, the predominance of oral information exchange, the presence of vested interests and the need to consider other people in authority and nonauthority relationships, the fuzziness of problems when they appear, and the structural and system characteristics at work.
3. Look at problems rather than at individual managers or work groups. Field studies indicate that important problems flowing through organizations involve many different people from many different parts of the organization—and even from the outside. Who becomes attached to what problem will vary, and understanding how and why this happens is a key research issue. The same problem may even change hands several times. Focusing on individuals or defined groups leaves out all of the others who coalesce around the decision streams. It also causes the observer to lose sight of what happens to the problem when it is away from the targeted individual(s).

Management education in decision making is in part dependent on the availability of research and therefore suffers from the same kinds of problems. Some of the things that might be taught, such as shepherding convoluted processes or guidelines for shooting from the hip, are elusive and little understood. Problem-solving/decision-making techniques are worth teaching, but a real effort must be made to point out the limited conditions under which they can be applied.

A more practical approach to training managers in decision making is to accept that there is no "quick fix." The mixture of skills, knowledge, and contacts underlying managerial actions must accumulate over time. The keys to this seem to lie in the judicious use of assignments, coupled with the opportunity to make mistakes and with the kind of support necessary for people to learn from their efforts. It is possible to assess many managerial strengths and weaknesses from *realistic* simulations of decision making, but awareness does not ensure learning. The challenge lies in facing real problems in a real context, and this is found on the firing line—not in a classroom. Career development, then, must take into account the variety of demands facing the managerial decision maker; it must also take advantage of assignments to teach, in moderate doses, the many skills that are required.

If organizations are to improve their decision processes, where should they begin? As our knowledge of decision making grows and the sophistication of training on and off the job increases, *individuals* will become better equipped to act in complex decision situations. But individuals seldom fully control the decision process and, even if they are skilled, organizational characteristics can negate their impact. Another place to begin improving managerial decision making is with the *organization's* values; systems and structures should be made consonant with these values. But this type of initiative will founder unless the organization is populated with individuals who have the requisite skills.

Actions at the individual and at the organizational levels, then, go hand in hand, but beyond that, the attempt to create such movement is but one instance of the types of processes described in this book. How does one know in the first place what the current state of decision-making practices is in an organization? Of the various aspects of managerial practice deemed in need of improvement, which get attention? What *kind* of attention is called for? Should the effort begin with the equivalent of little jabs designed to determine better what is involved? Or should the effort begin with a broad-based policy initiative that sets a convoluted process in motion. Whatever the effort made, how will the manager or organization discover the outcome, amid the press of other events and in light of prejudice to see the change effort favorably or unfavorably? We have come full circle: The process by which decision-making practice changes is basically the same process as that which is being changed. Organizations take action on this front in fundamentally the same way they take action on any other front—by doing whatever it takes.

# REFERENCES

ACKOFF, R. Management misinformation systems. *Management Science,* 1967, *14*(4), B147–B156.

ALDRICH, H. E. *Organizations and environments.* Englewood Cliffs, N.J.: Prentice-Hall, 1979.

ARGYRIS, C., & SCHON, D. A. *Theory in practice: Increasing professional effectiveness.* Washington, D.C.: Jossey-Bass, 1974.

ASHKENAS, R. N., & SCHAFFER, R. H. Managers can avoid wasting time. *Harvard Business Review,* 1982, *60*(3), 98–104.

BENNIS, W. *The unconscious conspiracy: Why leaders can't lead.* New York: AMACOM, 1976.

BENNIS, W. Leadership transforms vision into action. *Industry Week,* May 31, 1982, 54–56.

BENNIS, W., & NANUS, B. *Leaders: The strategies for taking charge.* New York: Harper & Row, 1985.

BERGER, P. L., & KELLNER, H. Marriage and the construction of reality. In H. P. Dreitzel (Ed.), *Recent sociology, No. 2: Patterns of communicative behavior.* New York: Macmillan, 1970.

BERGER, P. L., & LUCKMANN, T. *The social construction of reality: A treatise in the sociology of knowledge.* Garden City, N.Y.: Anchor, 1967.

BOULDING, K. E. *The image: Knowledge in life and society.* Ann Arbor: University of Michigan Press, 1966.

BROUNSTEIN, P., OSTROVE, N., & MILLS, J. Divergence of private evaluations of alternatives prior to choice. *Journal of Personality and Social Psychology,* 1979, *37*(11), 1957–1965.

BURNS, J. M. *Leadership.* New York: Harper & Row, 1978.

CADBURY, A. Ethical managers make their own rules. *Harvard Business Review,* 1987, *65*(5), 69–73.

CARTER, E. The behavioral theory of the firm and top-level corporate decisions. *Administrative Science Quarterly,* 1971, *16*(4), 413–428.

CHURCHILL, W. The hinge of fate. In *The second world war* (Vol. 4). New York: Bantam, 1962. (a)

CHURCHILL, W. Triumph and tragedy. In *The second world war* (Vol. 6). New York: Bantam, 1962. (b)

CLARK, T. D., JR., & SHRODE, W. A. Public-sector decision structures: An empirically based description. *Public Administration Review,* 1979, *39*(4), 343–354.

COHEN, M. D., & MARCH, J. *Leadership and ambiguity: The American college president.* New York: McGraw-Hill, 1974.

COHEN, M. D., MARCH, J. G., & OLSEN, J. P. A garbage can model of organizational choice. *Administrative Science Quarterly,* 1972, *17*, #1 1–25.

CONNOLLY, T. Diffuseness: An integrating principle. Invited paper at Joint National Meeting of ORSA, TIMS, and AIIE, Atlantic City, November 1972.

CONNOLLY, T. Uncertainty, action and competence: Some alternatives to omniscience in complex problem-solving. In S. Fiddle (Ed.), *Uncertainty: Social and behavioral dimensions.* New York: Praeger, 1980.

CONNOLLY, T., & WOLF, G. Deciding on decision strategies: Toward an enriched contingency model. In K. H. Chung (Ed.), *Proceedings,* Academy of Management Annual Meeting, San Diego, Calif., August 1981.

COSTELLO, T. W., & ZALKIND, S. S. Perception: Implications for administration. *Administrative Science Quarterly,* 1962, *7*, #2 218–235.

CYERT, R., DEGROOT, M., & HOLT, C. Capital allocation within a firm. *Behavioral Science,* 1979, *24*(5), 287–295.

CYERT, R., SIMON, H., & TROW, D. Observation of a business decision. *Journal of Business,* 1956, *29*, 237–248.

DE SEGUR, COUNT PHILIPE-PAUL. *Napoleon's Russian Campaign.* Translated from the French by J. David Townsend. Chicago: Time-Life Books, 1958.

DEARBORN, D. C., & SIMON, H. A. Selective perception: A note on the departmental identifications of executives. *Sociometry,* 1958, *21*, 140–144.

DILL, W. The varieties of administrative decisions. In H. Leavitt & L. Pondy (Eds.), *Readings in managerial psychology.* Chicago: University of Chicago, 1964, 457–473.

DIXON, N. *On the psychology of military incompetence.* New York: Basic Books, 1976.

DUBIN,R. Business behavior *behaviorally* viewed. In G. Strother (Ed.), *Social science approaches to business behavior.* Homewood, Ill.: Dorsey & Irwin, 1965, 11–55.

EDDY, P., POTTER, E., & PAGE, B. *Destination disaster.* New York: Quadrangle/The New York Times Book Co., 1976.

EINHORN, H. J., & HOGARTH, R. M. Decision making: Going forward in reverse. *Harvard Business Review*, 1987, *65*(1), 66–70.

ETZIONI, A. *The active society*. New York: Free Press, 1968.

FELDMAN, S. P. Secrecy, information, and politics: An essay on organizational decision making. *Human Relations*, 1988, *41*(1), 73–90.

FINK, S. A conversation with Shel Davis. *Exchange*, 1979, *4*(4), 12–18.

FISHMAN, K. D. *The computer establishment*. New York: Harper & Row, 1981.

FOX, J.M. *Executive qualities*. Reading, Mass.: Addison-Wesley, 1976.

FOX, F., & STAW, B. M. The trapped administrator: Effects of job insecurity and policy resistance upon commitment to a course of action. *Administrative Science Quarterly*, 1979, *24*(3), 449–471.

FROST, P. J., MITCHELL, V. F., & NORD, W. R. Air Force A-7D brake problem. In *Organizational reality*. Santa Monica, Calif.: Goodyear Publishing, 1978, p. 418.

GABARRO, J. J. When a new manager takes charge. *Harvard Business Review*, 1985, *63*(3), 110–123.

GABARRO, J. J. *The dynamics of taking charge*. Boston: Harvard Business School Press, 1987.

GALBRAITH, J. *Designing complex systems*. Reading, Mass.: Addison-Wesley, 1973.

GALBRAITH, J. Designing the innovating organization. *Organizational Dynamics*, Winter 1982, 5–25.

GERBASI, K., ZUCKERMAN, M., & REIS, H. Justice needs a new blindfold: A review of mock jury research. *Psychological Bulletin*, 1977, *84*(2), 323–345.

HALBERSTAM, D. *The best and the brightest*. New York: Fawcett Crest, 1969.

HAMBRICK, D. C. The top management team: Key to strategic success. *California Management Review*, 1987, *30*(1), 88–108.

HAMBRICK, D. C., AND MASON, P. A. Upper echelons: The organization as a reflection of its top managers. *Academy of Management Review*, 1984, *9*(2), 193–206.

HAYES, R. H. Why strategic planning goes awry. *New York Times*, April 20, 1986, sec. 3, p. 2.

HEINLEIN, R. A. *Farnham's freehold*. New York: Signet, 1964.

HOGARTH, R. M. Beyond discrete biases: Functional and dysfunctional aspects of judgmental heuristics. *Psychological Bulletin*, 1981, *90*, 197–217.

HOGARTH, R. M., & MAKRIDAKIS, S. Forecasting and planning: An evaluation. *Management Science*, 1981, *27*(2), 115–138.

ILGEN, D., FISHER, C., & TAYLOR, M. Consequences of individual feedback on behavior in organizations. *Journal of Applied Psychology*, 1979, *64*(4), 349–371.

ISENBERG, D. J. How senior managers think. *Harvard Business Review*, 1984, *62*(6), 81–90.

ISENBERG, D. J. Thinking and managing: A verbal protocol analysis of managerial problem solving. *Academy of Management Journal*, 1986, *29*(4), 775–788.

ISENBERG, D. J. The tactics of opportunism. *Harvard Business Review*, 1987, *65*(2), 92–97.

JAMES, H. *The golden bowl*. New York: Penguin, 1967. (First published in 1904.)

JAMES, W. *Psychology*. Cleveland: Fine Editions Press, 1948.

JANIS, I. L., & MANN, L. *Decision making: A psychological analysis of conflict, choice and commitment*. New York: Free Press, 1977.

KANTER, R. *Men and women of the corporation.* New York: Basic Books, 1977.

KAPLAN, R. E. An executive's reflections on executives: An interview with Roger T. Kelley. *Issues & Observations.* Greensboro, N.C.: Center for Creative Leadership, 1982, *2*, 1–4.

KAPLAN, R. E. *The warp and woof of the general manager's job* (Tech. Rep. No. 27). Greensboro, N.C.: Center for Creative Leadership, 1986.

KAPLAN, R. E. *The expansive executive.* Greensboro, N.C.: Center for Creative Leadership, 1989.

KAPLAN, R. E., DRATH, W. H., & KOFODIMOS, J. R. *High hurdles: The challenge of executive self-development.* Greensboro, N.C.: Center for Creative Leadership, 1984.

KAPLAN R. E., LOMBARDO, M. M., & MAZIQUE, M. S. *A mirror for managers: Using simulation to develop management teams* (Tech. Rep. No. 23). Greensboro, N.C.: Center for Creative Leadership, 1983.

KAPLAN, R. E., & MAZIQUE, M. S. *Trade routes: The manager's network of relationships* (Tech. Rep. No. 22). Greensboro, N.C.: Center for Creative Leadership, 1983.

KELLY, G. A. *A Theory of personality: A psychology of personal constructs.* New York: Norton, 1955.

KERR, S. On the folly of rewarding A, while hoping for B. *Academy of Management Journal,* 1975, *18*, 769–783.

KIDDER, T. *The soul of a new machine.* Boston: Little, Brown, 1981.

KISSINGER, H. A. *White house years.* Boston: Little, Brown, 1979.

KOTTER, J. P. *Power in management.* New York: AMACOM, 1979.

KOTTER, J. P. *The general managers.* New York: Free Press, 1982.

KOTTER, J. P., & LAWRENCE, P. R. *Mayors in action: Five approaches to urban governance.* New York: Wiley, 1976.

KOUZES, J. M, & POSNER, B. Z. *The leadership challenge.* San Francisco: Jossey-Bass, 1987.

LIEBERMAN, S. The effects of changes in roles in the attitudes of role occupants. *Human Relations,* 1954, *9*, 385–402.

LIVINGSTON, J. S. Myth of the well-educated manager. *Harvard Business Review,* 1971, *49*(1), 79–89.

LYLES, M., & MITROFF, I. Organizational problem formulation: An empirical study. *Administrative Science Quarterly,* 1980, *25*(1), 102–119.

MANCHESTER, W. *American Caesar.* New York: Dell, 1978.

MARCH, J. G., & OLSEN, J. P. *Ambiguity and choice in organizations.* Bergen, Norway: Universitetsforlaget, 1976.

MARCH, J. G., & SHAPIRA, Z. Managerial perspectives on risk and risk taking. *Management Science,* 1987, *33*(11), 1404–1418.

MARCH, J. G., & SIMON, H. A. *Organizations.* New York: Wiley, 1958.

MCCALL, M. W., JR., & LOMBARDO, M. *Looking Glass, Inc.: An organizational simulation* (Tech. Rep. No. 12). Greensboro, N.C.: Center for Creative Leadership, 1978.

MCCALL, M. W., JR., & LOMBARDO, M. M. *Off the track: Why and how successful executives get derailed* (Tech. Rep. No. 21). Greensboro, N.C.: Center for Creative Leadership, 1983.

McCALL, M. W., JR., LOMBARDO, M. M., & MORRISON, A. M. *The lessons of experience.* Lexington, Mass.: Lexington Books, 1988.

McCALL, M. W., JR., MORRISON, A. M., & HANNAN, R. L. *Studies of managerial work: Results and methods* (Tech. Re. No. 9). Greensboro, N.C.: Center for Creative Leadership, 1978.

MINTZBERG, H. *The nature of managerial work.* New York: Harper & Row, 1973.

MINTZBERG, H. Patterns in strategy formation. *Management Science,* 1978, *24*(9), 934–948.

MINTZBERG, H. Crafting strategy. *Harvard Business Review,* 1987, *65*(4), 66–75.

MINTZBERG, H., RAISINGHANI, D., & THEORET, A. The structure of "unstructured" decision processes. *Administrative Science Quarterly,* 1976, *21*, 246–275.

MIRVIS, P., & BERG, D. (EDS.). *Failures in organization development and change.* New York: Wiley, 1977.

MITROFF, I. I. Crisis management: Cutting through the confusion. *Sloan Management Review,* Winter 1988, 15–20.

MITROFF, I. I., SHRIVASTAVA, P., & UDWADIA, F. Effective crisis management. *Academy of Management Executive,* November 1987, 283–292.

MORTON THIOKOL: Reflections on the shuttle disaster. *Business Week,* March 14, 1988, 82–91.

MOSLEY, L. *Blood relations: The rise and fall of the du Ponts of Delaware.* New York: Atheneum, 1980.

MURRAY, E., JR. Strategic choice as a negotiated outcome. *Management Science,* 1978, *24*(9), 960–972.

NEWHOUSE, J. A sporting game (Part IV). *New Yorker,* July 5, 1982.

O'REILLY, C. A., III. Individuals and information overload in organizations: Is more necessarily better? *Academy of Management Journal,* 1980, *23*(4), 684–696.

OUCHI, W. The broad career path of Japanese executives. *Wall Street Journal,* April 6, 1981.

PASCALE, R. T., & ATHOS, A. G. *The art of Japanese management: Applications for American executives.* New York: Simon and Schuster, 1981.

PATCHEN, M. The locus and basis of influence on organizational decisions. *Organizational Behavior and Human Performance,* 1974, *11*, 195–221.

PATTON, G., JR. *War as I knew it.* Boston: Houghton Mifflin, 1947.

PERROW, C. *Complex organizations.* Glenview, Ill.: Scott, Foresman, 1972.

PETERS, T. J., & WATERMAN, R. H., JR. *In search of excellence.* New York: Harper & Row, 1982.

PFEFFER, J. The ambiguity of leadership. In M. W. McCall, Jr., & M. M. Lombardo (Eds.), *Leadership: Where else can we go?* Durham, N.C.: Duke University Press, 1978.

POUNDS, W. The process of problem finding. *Industrial Management Review* (now *Sloan Management Review*), 1969, *11*(1), 1–19.

RAYMOND, R. C. Betting on new technologies. In J. R. Bright (Ed.), *Technological planning on the corporate level.* Boston: Division of Research, Harvard Business School, 1962.

READ, W. H. Upward communication in industrial hierarchies. *Human Relations,* 1962, *15*, 3–15.

ROBINSON, J. A., HERMANN, C. F., & HERMAN, M. G. Search under crisis in political gaming and simulation. In D. G. Pruitt & R. C. Snyder (Eds.), *Theory and research on the causes of war.* Englewood Cliffs, N.J.: Prentice-Hall, 1969.

ROSS, L. The intuitive psychologist and his shortcomings: Distortions in the attribution process. In L. Berkowitz, (Ed.), *Advances in experimental social psychology* (Vol. 10). New York: Academic Press, 1977.

SALANCIK, G. Commitment and the control of organizational behavior and belief. In B. Staw & G. Salancik (Eds.), *New directions in organizational behavior.* Chicago: St. Clair, 1977, 1–54.

SAYLES, L. *Leadership.* New York: McGraw-Hill, 1979.

SAYLES, L. R., & CHANDLER, M. K. *Managing large systems: Organizations for the future.* New York: Harper & Row, 1971.

SCHON, D. A. *The reflective practitioner: How professionals think in action.* New York: Basic Books, 1983.

SHUMWAY, C., MAHER, P., BAKER, M., SOUDER, W., RUBINSTEIN, A., & GALLANT, A. Diffuse decision-making in hierarchical organizations: An empirical examination. *Management Science,* 1975, *21*(6), 697–707.

SIMON, H. Information processing models of cognition. *Annual Review of Psychology,* 1979, *30,* 363–396.

SLOVIC, P., FISCHOFF, B., & LICHTENSTEIN, S. Behavioral decision theory. In M. Rosenzweig & L. Porter (Eds.), *Annual Review of Psychology,* 1977, *28,* 1–39. Palo Alto, Calif.: Annual Reviews.

SMITH, R. *Corporations in crisis.* Garden City, N.Y.: Doubleday, 1963.

SMITH, D., & ALEXANDER, R. *Fumbling the future.* New York: Morrow, 1988.

SPEER, A. *Inside the Third Reich,* New York: Avon Books, 1970.

STAW, B. M. Knee-deep in the big muddy: A study of escalating commitment to a chosen course of action. *Organizational Behavior and Human Performance,* 1976, *16,* 27–44.

STAW, B. M., & ROSS, J. Behavior in escalation situations: Antecedents, prototypes, and solutions. In *Research in organizational behavior* (Vol. 9). Greenwich, Conn.: JAI Press, 1987, 39–78.

STAW, B. M., & ROSS, J. Knowing when to pull the plug. *Harvard Business Review,* 1987, *65*(2), 68–74.

STEWART, R. Managerial agendas—Reactive or proactive? *Organizational Dynamics,* Autumn 1979.

STEWART, R. *Choices for the manager.* Englewood Cliffs, N.J.: Prentice-Hall, 1982.

STOKES, R., & HEWITT, J. Aligning actions. *American Sociological Review,* 1976, *41*(5), 838–849.

SVENSON, O. Process descriptions of decision making. *Organizational Behavior and Human Performance,* 1979, *23,* 86–112.

TAYLOR, D. Decision making and problem solving. In J. March (Ed.), *Handbook of organizations.* Chicago: Rand McNally, 1965, 48–86.

THOMAS, L. *The medusa and the snail.* New York: Viking Press, 1979.

TOLKIEN, J. The two towers. In *Lord of the rings* (Part 2). Boston: Houghton Mifflin, 1965.

TORBERT, W. R. *Managing the corporate dream: Restructuring for long-term success.* Homewood, Ill.: Dow Jones-Irwin, 1987.

TUCHMAN, B. An inquiry into the persistence of unwisdom in government. *Esquire,* 1980, *93*(5), 25–31.

TUCHMAN, G. *Making news: A study in the construction of reality.* New York: Free Press, 1978.

WEBB, E., & WEICK, K. E. Unobtrusive measures in organizational theory: A reminder. *Administrative Science Quarterly,* 1979, *24,* 650–659.

WEICK, K. *The social psychology of organizing* (2nd ed.). Reading, Mass.: Addison-Wesley, 1979.

WHETTON, D. Organizational decline: A neglected topic in organizational science. *Academy of Management Review,* 1980, *5*(4), 577–588.

WILENSKY, H. *Organizational intelligence: Knowledge and policy in government and industry.* New York: Basic Books, 1967.

WITTE, E. Field research on complex decision making processes—the phase theorem. *International Studies of Management and Organization,* 1972, *2,* 156–182.

WRIGHT, J. P. *On a clear day you can see General Motors.* New York: Avon, 1979.

# *NOTES*

## PREFACE

[1]W. Bennis, "Leadership Transforms Vision into Action," *Industry Week,* May 31, 1982, pp. 54–56.

[2]T. Connolly, "Uncertainty, Action, and Competence: Some Alternatives to Omniscience in Complex Problem-Solving," in *Uncertainty: Social and Behavioral Dimensions,* ed. S. Fiddle (New York: Praeger, 1980).

[3]J. M. Burns, *Leadership* (New York: Harper & Row, 1978), p. 379.

[4]Ibid.

[5]R. M. Hogarth, "Beyond Discrete Biases: Functional and Dysfunctional Aspects of Judgmental Heuristics," *Psychological Bulletin,* 90, no. 2 (1981), 198.

[6]R. T. Pascale and A. G. Athos, *The Art of Japanese Management: Applications for American Executives* (New York: Simon & Schuster, 1981), p. 110.

[7]L. Sayles, *Leadership* (New York: McGraw-Hill, 1979), pp. 12–18.

[8]See, for example, M. W. McCall, Jr., A. M. Morrison, and R. L. Hannan, *Studies of Managerial Work: Results and Methods* (Tech. Rep. No. 9) (Greensboro, N.C.: Center for Creative Leadership, 1978).

[9]K. Weick, *The Social Psychology of Organizing,* 2nd ed. (Reading, Mass.: Addison-Wesley, 1979).

[10]H. Mintzberg, *The Nature of Managerial Work* (New York: Harper & Row, 1973); Sayles, *Leadership.*

[11]H. Mintzberg, "Patterns in Strategy Formation," *Management Science,* 24, no. 9 (1978), 934–948.

# CHAPTER 1

[1]P. Eddy, E. Potter, and B. Page, *Destination Disaster* (New York: Quadrangle/The New York Times Book Co., 1976), pp. 245–246.

[2]Eddy, Potter, and Page, *Destination Disaster*.

[3]W. Churchill, "Triumph and Tragedy," in *The Second World War,* Vol. 6 (New York: Bantam, 1962), p. 546.

[4]N. Dixon, *On the Psychology of Military Incompetence* (New York: Basic Books, 1976), p. 147.

[5]"Morton Thiokol: Reflections on the Shuttle Disaster," *Business Week*, March 14, 1988, pp. 82–91; I. I. Mitroff, P. Shrivastava, and F. Udwadia, "Effective Crisis Management," *Academy of Management Executive,* 1, no. 4 (1987), 283–292.

[6]President's Commission findings as quoted in "Morton Thiokol," p. 82.

[7]I. I. Mitroff, "Crisis Management: Cutting through the Confusion," *Sloan Management Review,* 29, no. 2 (1988), 20.

[8]L. Sayles, *Leadership* (New York: McGraw-Hill, 1979), p. 15.

[9]Sayles, *Leadership*.

[10]E. Witte, "Field Research on Complex Decision Making Processes—The Phase Theorem," *International Studies of Management and Organization,* 2 (1972), 156–182.

[11]See K. Gerbasi, M. Zuckerman, and H. Reis, "Justice Needs a New Blindfold: A Review of Mock Jury Research," *Psychological Bulletin*, 84, no. 2 (1977), 323–345.

[12]H. Mintzberg, "Crafting Strategy," *Harvard Business Review*, 65, no. 4 (1987), 68.

[13]D. J. Isenberg, "How Senior Managers Think," *Harvard Business Review*, 62, no. 6 (1984), 89.

[14]D. A. Schon, *The Reflective Practitioner: How Professionals Think in Action* (New York: Basic Books, 1983), p. 241.

[15]W. R. Torbert, *Managing the Corporate Dream: Restructuring for Long-Term Success* (Homewood, Ill.: Dow Jones-Irwin, 1987).

# CHAPTER 2

[1]For example, W. Pounds, "The Process of Problem Finding," *Industrial Management Review* (now *Sloan Management Review*), 11, no. 1 (1969), 1–19; J. S. Livingston, "Myth of the Well-Educated Manager," *Harvard Business Review*, 49, no. 1 (1971), 79–89; M. Lyles and I. Mitroff, "Organizational Problem Formulation: An Empirical Study," *Administrative Science Quarterly*, 25, no. 1 (1980), 102–119; J. J. Gabarro, *The Dynamics of Taking Charge* (Boston: Harvard Business School Press, 1987).

[2]H. Mintzberg, *The Nature of Managerial Work* (New York: Harper & Row, 1973); L. Sayles, *Leadership* (New York: McGraw-Hill, 1979).

[3]R.E. Kaplan, *The Warp and Woof of the General Manager's Job* (Tech. Rep. No. 27) (Greensboro, N.C.: Center for Creative Leadership, 1986).

[4]D. J. Isenberg, "How Senior Managers Think," *Harvard Business Review*, 62, no. 6 (1984), 83.

[5]Isenberg, "Senior Managers"; Kaplan, *Warp and Woof.*

[6]W. R. Torbert, *Managing the Corporate Dream: Restructuring for Long-Term Success* (Homewood, Ill.: Dow Jones-Irwin, 1987).

[7]Pounds, "Problem Finding," p. 5.

[8]Ibid., p. 7.

[9]Ibid., p. 8.

[10]E. Carter, "The Behavioral Theory of the Firm and Top-Level Corporate Deicsions," *Administrative Science Quarterly*, 16, no. 4 (1971), 413–428.

[11]H. Wilensky, *Organizational Intelligence: Knowledge and Policy in Government and Industry* (New York: Basic Books, 1967), p. 41.

[12]M. W. McCall, Jr., A. M. Morrison, and R. L. Hannan, *Studies of Managerial Work: Results and Methods* (Tech. Rep. No. 9) (Greensboro: N.C.: Center for Creative Leadership, 1978).

[13]For example, C. A. O'Reilly III, "Individuals and Information Overload in Organizations: Is More Necessarily Better? *Academy of Management Journal,* 23, no. 4 (1980), 684–696.

[14]R. Ackoff, "Management Misinformation Systems," *Management Science,* 14, no. 4 (1967), B147–B156.

[15]R. B. Hogarth and S. Makridakis, "Forecasting and Planning: An Evaluation," *Management Science,* 27, no. 2 (1981), 115–138.

[16]Ibid., p. 130.

[17]Pounds, "Problem Finding," p. 9.

[18]J. Galbraith, *Designing Complex Systems* (Reading, Mass.: Addison-Wesley, 1973).

[19]J. P. Kotter, *The General Managers* (New York: Free Press, 1982), pp. 14–15.

[20]Galbraith, *Designing Complex Systems,* p. 11.

[21]Wilensky, *Organizational Intelligence,* p. 48.

[22]W. H. Read, "Upward Communication in Industrial Hierarchies," *Human Relations,* 15 no. 1 (1962), 3–15.

[23]Lyles and Mitroff, "Organizational Problem Formulation," p. 113.

[24]Wilensky, *Organizational Intelligence,* p. 43.

[25]Kotter, *General Managers.*

[26]W. Bennis, *The Unconscious Conspiracy: Why Leaders Can't Lead* (New York: AMACOM, 1976), p. 106.

[27]D. Halberstam, *The Best and the Brightest* (New York: Fawcett Crest, 1969), p. 336.

[28]Kotter, *General Managers.*

[29]Wilensky, *Organizational Intelligence.*

[30]L. R. Sayles and M. K. Chandler, *Managing Large Systems: Organizations for the Future* (New York: Harper & Row, 1971).

[31]T. J. Peters and R. H. Waterman, Jr., *In Search of Excellence* (New York: Harper & Row, 1982), p. 281.

[32]Ibid., p. 260.

[33]Hogarth and Makridakis, "Forecasting and Planning."

[34]G. Patton, Jr., *War As I Knew It* (Boston: Houghton Mifflin, 1947).

[35]H. Mintzberg, "Crafting Strategy," *Harvard Business Review,* 65, no. 4 (1987), 66–75.

[36]R. C. Raymond, "Betting on New Technologies," in *Technological Planning on the Corporate Level,* ed. J. R. Bright (Boston: Division of Research, Harvard Business School, 1962).

[37]H. Simon, "Information Processing Models of Cognition," *Annual Review of Psychology,* 30 (1979), 363–396.

[38]J. G. March and H. A. Simon, *Organizations* (New York: Wiley, 1958).

[39]Simon, "Information Processing Models," p. 368.

[40]J. G. March and J. P. Olsen, *Ambiguity and Choice in Organizations* (Bergen, Norway: Universitetsforlaget, 1976).

[41]Hogarth and Makridakis, "Forecasting and Planning."

[42]G. A. Kelly, *A Theory of Personality: A Psychology of Personal Constructs* ( New York: Norton, 1955).

[43]D. C. Dearborn and H. A. Simon, "Selective Perception: A Note on the Departmental Identifications of Executives," *Sociometry,* 21 (1958), 140–144.

[44]J. J. Gabarro, "When A New Manager Takes Charge," *Harvard Business Review,* 63, no. 3 (1985), 116.

[45]W. Ouchi, "The Broad Career Path of Japanese Executives," *Wall Street Journal,* April, 6, 1981.

[46]S. Lieberman, "The Effects of Changes in Roles in the Attitudes of Role Occupants," *Human Relations,* 9 (1954), 385–402.

[47]R. Kanter, *Men and Women of the Corporation* (New York: Basic Books, 1977).

[48]T. W. Costello and S. S. Zalkind, "Perception: Implications for Administration," *Administrative Science Quarterly,* 7 (1962), 227.

[49]I. L. Janis and L. Mann, *Decision Making: A Psychological Analysis of Conflict, Choice, and Commitment* (New York: Free Press, 1977), p. 121.

[50]Lyles and Mitroff, "Organizational Problem Formulation," p. 116.

[51]K. E. Boulding, *The Image: Knowledge in Life and Society* (Ann Arbor: University of Michigan Press, 1966).

[52]Sayles, *Leadership,* p. 129.

[53]Mintzberg, "Crafting Strategy," p. 74.

[54]Janis and Mann, *Decision Making.*

[55]H. James, *The Golden Bowl* (New York: Penguin, 1967). (First published in 1904.)

[56]McCall, Morrison, and Hannan, *Studies of Managerial Work.*

[57]P. L. Berger and T. Luckmann, *The Social Construction of Reality: A Treatise in the Sociology of Knowledge* (Garden City, N.Y.: Anchor, 1967); P. L. Berger and H. Kellner, "Marriage and the Construction of Reality," in *Recent Sociology, No. 2: Patterns of Communicative Behavior,* ed. H. P. Dreitzel (New York: Macmillan, 1970).

[58]S. P. Feldman, "Secrecy, Information, and Politics: An Essay on Organizational Decision Making," *Human Relations,* 41, no. 1 (1988), 73–90.

[59]P. J. Frost, V. F. Mitchell, and W. R. Nord, "Air Force A-7D Brake Problem," in *Organizational Reality* (Santa Monica, Calif.: Goodyear Publishing, 1978), p. 425.

[60]Pounds, "Problem Finding."

[61]Lyles and Mitroff, "Organizational Problem Formulation."

[62]P. Eddy, E. Potter, and B. Page, *Destination Disaster* (New York: Quadrangle/The New York Times Book Co., 1976).

[63]I. I. Mitroff, P. Shrivastava, and F. Udwadia, "Effective Crisis Management," *Academy of Management Executive,* 1, no. 4 (1987), 283–292.

[64]H. E. Aldrich, *Organizations and Environments* (Englewood Cliffs, N.J.: Prentice-Hall, 1979).

[65]For example, Kotter, *General Managers.*

[66]Ibid.

[67]Ibid.; Gabarro, *Dynamics of Taking Charge.*

[68]R. E. Kaplan, *The Expansive Executive* (Greensboro, N.C.: Center for Creative Leadership, 1989).

[69]Ibid.

[70]D. A. Schon, *The Reflective Practitioner: How Professionals Think in Action* (New York: Basic Books, 1983), p. 269.

[71]Mintzberg, "Crafting Strategy," p. 74.

[72]I. I. Mitroff, "Crisis Management: Cutting through the Confusion," *Sloan Management Review,* 29, no. 2 (1988), 15–20.

[73]Isenberg, "Senior Managers," p. 88.

[74]Torbert, *Managing the Corporate Dream.*

[75]Ibid., p. 160.

# CHAPTER 3

[1]J. M. Kouzes and B. Z. Posner, *The Leadership Challenge* (San Francisco: Jossey-Bass, 1987), p. 79.

[2]W. Bennis and B. Nanus, *Leaders: The Strategies for Taking Charge* (New York: Harper & Row, 1985), p. 89.

[3]J. P. Kotter, *The General Managers* (New York: Free Press, 1982), pp. 60–61.

[4]W. Pounds, "The Process of Problem Finding," *Industrial Management Review* (now *Sloan Management Review*), 11, no. 1 (1969), 10.

[5]For example, H. Mintzberg, *The Nature of Managerial Work* (New York: Harper & Row, 1973).

[6]M. Cohen and J. March, *Leadership and Ambiguity: The American College President* (New York: McGraw-Hill, 1974).

[7]C. Perrow, *Complex Organizations* (Glenview, Ill.: Scott, Foresman, 1972).

[8]R. Stewart, "Managerial Agendas—Reactive or Proactive?" *Organizational Dynamics, 8*, no. 2 (1979), 34–47; J. P. Kotter and P. R. Lawrence, *Mayors in Action: Five Approaches to Urban Governance* (New York: Wiley, 1976).

[9]Kotter, *General Managers.*

[10]T. J. Peters, and R. H. Waterman, Jr., *In Search of Excellence* (New York: Harper & Row, 1982), p. 68.

[11]Bennis and Nanus, *Leaders;* Kouzes and Posner, *Leadership Challenge.*

[12]M. D. Cohen, J. G. March, and J. P. Olsen, "A Garbage Can Model of Organizational Choice," *Administrative Science Quarterly,* 17, no. 1 (1972), 1–25.

[13]L. Thomas, *The Medusa and the Snail* (New York: Viking Press, 1979).

[14]T. D. Clark, Jr., and W. A. Shrode, "Public-Sector Decision Structures: An Empirically Based Description," *Public Administration Review,* 39, no. 4 (1979), 343–354.

[15]M. Lyles and I. Mitroff, "Organizational Problem Formulation: An Empirical Study," *Administrative Science Quarterly,* 25, no. 1 (1980), 102–119; H. Mintzberg, D. Raisinghani, and A. Theoret, "The Structure of 'Unstructured' Decision Processes," *Administrative Science Quarterly,* 21, no. 2 (1976), 246–275.

[16]Cohen and March, *Leadership and Ambiguity;* Cohen, March, and Olsen, "Garbage Can Model."

[17]W. Dill, "The Varieties of Administrative Decisions," in *Readings in Managerial Psychology,* ed. H. Leavitt and L. Pondy (Chicago: University of Chicago Press, 1964), pp. 457–473.

[18]Lyles and Mitroff, "Organizational Problem Formulation."

[19]Mintzberg, Raisinghani, and Theoret, " 'Unstructured' Decision Processes."

[20]P. Brounstein, N. Ostrove, and J. Mills, "Divergence of Private Evaluations of Alternatives Prior to Choice," *Journal of Personality and Social Psychology,* 37, no. 11 (1979), 1957–1965.

[21]For example, Pounds, "Problem Finding"; R. Cyert, M. DeGroot, and C. Holt, "Capital Allocation within a Firm," *Behavioral Science,* 24, no. 5 (1979), 287–295.

[22]R. M. Hogarth, "Beyond Discrete Biases: Functional and Dysfunctional Aspects of Judgmental Heuristics," *Psychological Bulletin,* 90, no. 2 (1981), 197–217.

[23]R. N. Ashkenas and R. H. Schaffer, "Managers Can Avoid Wasting Time," *Harvard Business Review,* 60, no. 3 (1982), 98–104.

[24]L. Mosley, *Blood Relations: The Rise and Fall of the du Ponts of Delaware* (New York: Atheneum, 1980), p. 212.

[25]J. Galbraith, "Designing the Innovating Organization," *Organizational Dynamics,* 10, no. 3 (1982), 6.

[26]D. Smith and R. Alexander, *Fumbling the Future* (New York: Morrow, 1988).

[27]Peters and Waterman, *In Search of Excellence,* p. 115.

[28]R. E. Kaplan and M. S. Mazique, *Trade Routes: The Manager's Network of Relationships* (Tech. Rep. No. 22) (Greensboro, N.C.: Center for Creative Leadership, 1983).

[29]Cyert, DeGroot, and Holt, "Capital Allocation"; L. Sayles, *Leadership* (New York: McGraw-Hill, 1979).

[30]Clark and Shrode, "Public-Sector Decision Structures."

[31]Pounds, "Problem Finding."

[32]For a review of such studies, see M. W. McCall, Jr., A. M. Morrison, and R. L. Hannan, *Studies of Managerial Work: Results and Methods* (Tech. Rep. No. 9) (Greensboro, N.C.: Center for Creative Leadership, 1978).

[33]For example, Lyles and Mitroff, "Organizational Problem Formulation."

[34]A. Cadbury, "Ethical Managers Make Their Own Rules," *Harvard Business Review*, 65, no. 5 (1987), 69–73.

[35]H. Simon, "Information Processing Models of Cognition," *Annual Review of Psychology*, 30 (1979), 363–396.

[36]Peters and Waterman, *In Search of Excellence*, p. 73.

[37]C. Argyris and D. A. Schon, *Theory in Practice: Increasing Professional Effectiveness* (Washington, D.C.: Jossey-Bass, 1974).

[38]M. Patchen, "The Locus and Basis of Influence on Organizational Decisions," *Organizational Behavior and Human Performance*, 11, no. 2 (1974), 195–221.

[39]R. Cyert, H. Simon, and D. Trow, "Observation of a Business Decision," *Journal of Business*, 29 (1956), 237–248.

[40]Mintzberg, Raisinghani, and Theoret, " 'Unstructured' Decision Processes."

[41]P. Slovic, B. Fischoff, and S. Lichtenstein, "Behavioral Decision Theory," *Annual Review of Psychology*, 28 (1977), 1–39.

[42]Pounds, "Problem Finding."

[43]Clark and Shrode, "Public-Sector Decision Structures."

[44]D. J. Isenberg, "How Senior Managers Think," *Harvard Business Review*, 62, no. 6 (1984), 81–90.

[45]Cyert, DeGroot, and Holt, "Capital Allocation."

[46]Peters and Waterman, *In Search of Excellence*.

[47]Stewart, "Managerial Agendas."

[48]Ibid., p. 43.

[49]Lyles and Mitroff, "Organizational Problem Formulation"; Mintzberg, Raisinghani, and Theoret, " 'Unstructured' Decision Processes"; I. I. Mitroff, "Crisis Management: Cutting through the Confusion," *Sloan Management Review*, 29, no. 2 (1988), 15–20.

[50]Pounds, "Problem Finding."

[51]Clark and Shrode, "Public-Sector Decision Structures."

[52]W. James, *Psychology* (Cleveland: Fine Editions Press, 1948).

[53]Pounds, "Problem Finding."

[54]E. Webb and K. E. Weick, "Unobtrusive Measures in Organizational Theory: A Reminder," *Administrative Science Quarterly*, 24, no. 4 (1979), 650–659.

[55]E. Witte, "Field Research on Complex Decision Making Processes—The Phase Theorem," *International Studies of Management and Organization*, 2 (1972), 156–182.

[56]M. W. McCall, Jr., and M. Lombardo, *Looking Glass, Inc.: An Organizational Simulation* (Tech. Rep. No. 12) (Greensboro, N.C.: Center for Creative Leadership, 1978).

[57]Mintzberg, Raisinghani, and Theoret, " 'Unstructured' Decision Processes."

[58]Mitroff, "Cutting through the Confusion," p. 15.

[59]Pounds, "Problem Finding."

[60]T. Kidder, *The Soul of a New Machine* (Boston: Little, Brown, 1981).

[61]Peters and Waterman, *In Search of Excellence*.

[62]D. Taylor, "Decision Making and Problem Solving," in *Handbook of Organizations*, ed. J. March (Chicago: Rand McNally, 1965), pp. 48–86; G. Salancik, "Commitment and the Control of Organizational Behavior and Belief," in *New Directions in Organizational Behavior*, ed. B. Staw and G. Salancik (Chicago: St. Clair, 1977), pp. 1–54.

[63]F. Fox and B. M. Staw, "The Trapped Administrator: Effects of Job Insecurity and Policy

Resistance upon Commitment to a Course of Action," *Administrative Science Quarterly,* 24, no. 3 (1979), 449–471.

[64]For a thorough review, see B. M. Staw and J. Ross, "Behavior in Escalation Situations: Antecedents, Prototypes, and Solutions," in *Research in Organizational Behavior,* Vol. 9 (Greenwich, Conn.: JAI Press, 1987), 39–78.

[65]W. Churchill, "The Hinge of Fate," in *The Second World War,* Vol 4 (New York: Bantam, 1962), p. 597.

[66]Stewart, "Managerial Agendas."

[67]D. J. Isenberg, "The Tactics of Opportunism," *Harvard Business Review,* 65, no. 2 (1987), 92.

[68]Ibid.

[69]Peters and Waterman, *In Search of Excellence,* p. 75.

[70]Kotter, *General Managers.*

[71]Stewart, "Managerial Agendas."

[72]Kotter, *General Managers.*

[73]Ibid.

[74]Ibid.

[75]B. M. Staw and J. Ross, "Behavior in Escalation Situations: Antecedents, Prototypes, and Solutions," in *Research in Organizational Behavior,* Vol. 9 (Greenwich, Conn.: JAI Press, 1987).

[76]H. Mintzberg, "Crafting Strategy," *Harvard Business Review,* 65, no. 4 (1987), 66–75.

[77]D. C. Hambrick and P. A. Mason, "Upper Echelons: The Organization as a Reflection of Its Top Managers," *Academy of Management Review,* 9, no. 2 (1984), 193–206.

# CHAPTER 4

[1]R. A. Heinlein, *Farnham's Freehold* (New York: Signet, 1964), p. 94.

[2]T. J. Peters and R. H. Waterman, Jr., *In Search of Excellence* (New York: Harper & Row, 1982), p. 150.

[3]H. Mintzberg, D. Raisinghani, and A. Theoret, "The Structure of 'Unstructured' Decision Processes," *Administrative Science Quarterly,* 21, no. 2 (1976), 246.

[4]E. Carter, "The Behavioral Theory of the Firm and Top-Level Corporate Decisions," *Administrative Science Quarterly,* 16, no. 4 (1971), 426.

[5]K. Gerbasi, M. Zuckerman, and H. Reis, "Justice Needs a New Blindfold: A Review of Mock Jury Research," *Psychological Bulletin,* 84, no. 2 (1977), 323–345.

[6]Carter, "Behavioral Theory."

[7]C. Shumway et al., "Diffuse Decision-Making in Hierarchical Organizations: An Empirical Examination," *Management Science,* 21, no. 6 (1975), 697–707.

[8]Mintzberg, Raisinghani, and Theoret, " 'Unstructured' Decision Processes."

[9]A. Speer, *Inside the Third Reich* (New York: Avon Books, 1970), p. 394.

[10]A. Etzioni, *The Active Society* (New York: Free Press, 1968), p. 301.

[11]R. Dubin, "Business Behavior *Behaviorally* Viewed," in *Social Science Approaches to Business Behavior,* ed. G. Strother (Homewood, Ill.: Dorsey & Irwin, 1965), p. 30.

[12]Mintzberg, Raisinghani, and Theoret, " 'Unstructured' Decision Processes."

[13]J. P. Kotter, *The General Managers* (New York: Free Press, 1982).

[14]D. J. Isenberg, "How Senior Managers Think," *Harvard Business Review,* 62, no. 6 (1984), 81–90.

[15]Kotter, *General Managers.*

[16]J. P. Kotter, *Power in Management* (New York: AMACOM, 1979), p. 42.

[17]T. D. Clark, Jr., and W. A. Shrode, "Public-Sector Decision Structures: An Empirically Based Description," *Public Administration* Review, 39, no. 4 (1979), 348.

[18]Kotter, *General Managers,* p. 14.

[19]Peters and Waterman, *In Search of Excellence.*

[20]L. R. Sayles and M. K. Chandler, *Managing Large Systems: Organizations for the Future* (New York: Harper & Row, 1971), p. 219.

[21]J. P. Wright, *On a Clear Day You Can See General Motors* (New York: Avon, 1979).

[22]J. A. Robinson, C. F. Hermann, and M. G. Herman, "Search under Crisis in Political Gaming and Simulation," in *Theory and Research on the Causes of War,* ed. D. G. Pruitt and R. C. Synder (Englewood Cliffs, N.J.: Prentice Hall, 1969).

[23]J. G. March and H. A. Simon, *Organizations* (New York: Wiley, 1958).

[24]Mintzberg, Raisinghani, and Theoret, " 'Unstructured' Decision Processes"; R. Cyert, M. DeGroot, and C. Holt, "Capital Allocation within a Firm," *Behavioral Science,* 24, no. 5 (1979), 287–295.

[25]Mintzberg, Raisinghani, and Theoret, " 'Unstructured' Decision Processes," p. 250.

[26]T. Connolly and G. Wolf, "Deciding on Decision Strategies: Toward an Enriched Contingency Model," in *Proceedings,* Academy of Management Annual Meetings, ed. K. H. Chung (San Diego: Academy of Management, August 1981), pp. 6–7.

[27]Etzioni, *Active Society.*

[28]F. Fox and B. M. Staw, "The Trapped Administrator: Effects of Job Insecurity and Policy Resistance upon Commitment to a Course of Action," *Administrative Science Quarterly,* 24, no. 3 (1979), 461.

[29]W. Bennis, *The Unconscious Conspiracy: Why Leaders Can't Lead* (New York: AMACOM, 1976), p. 103.

[30]I. I. Mitroff, "Crisis Management: Cutting through the Confusion," *Sloan Management Review,* 29, no. 2 (1988), 15–20.

[31]J. J. Gabarro, "When a New Manager Takes Charge," *Harvard Business Review,* 62, no. 3 (1985), 110–123.

[32]Ibid., p. 119.

[33]T. Connolly, "Diffuseness: An Integrating Principle" (invited paper at Joint National Meeting of ORSA, TIMS, and AIIE, Atlantic City, November 1972).

[34]H. Mintzberg, "Crafting Strategy," *Harvard Business Review,* 65, no. 4 (1987), 69.

[35]R. H. Hayes, "Why Strategic Planning Goes Awry," *The New York Times,* April 20, 1986, sec. 3, p. 2.

[36]Mintzberg, Raisinghani, and Theoret, " 'Unstructured' Decision Processes," p. 254.

[37]Ibid., p. 256.

[38]Ibid.

[39]Ibid.

[40]H. Minztberg, "Patterns in Strategy Formation," *Management Science,* 24, no. 9 (1978), 934–948.

[41]Dubin, "Business Behavior," p. 30.

[42]Sayles and Chandler, *Managing Large Systems,* p. 176.

[43]E. Murray, Jr., "Strategic Choice as a Negotiated Outcome," *Management Science,* 24, no. 9 (1978), 960–972.

[44]Peters and Waterman, *In Search of Excellence.*

[45]Sayles and Chandler, *Managing Large Systems,* p. 196.

[46]Mintzberg, Raisinghani, and Theoret, " 'Unstructured' Decision Processes."

[47]Isenberg, "Senior Managers."

[48]Kotter, *General Managers.*

[49]Peters and Waterman, *In Search of Excellence.*

[50]Sayles and Chandler, *Managing Large Systems,* p. 209.

[51]Isenberg, "Senior Managers."

[52]M. W. McCall, Jr., M. M. Lombardo, and A. M. Morrison, *The Lessons of Experience* (Lexington, Mass.: Lexington Books, 1988).

# CHAPTER 5

[1]R. Smith, *Corporations in Crisis* (Garden City, N.Y.: Doubleday, 1963), p. 73.

[2]L. Thomas, *The Medusa and the Snail* (New York: Viking Press, 1979), pp. 37–38.

[3]R. E. Kaplan, M. M. Lombardo, and M. S. Mazique, *A Mirror for Managers: Using Simulation to Develop Management Teams* (Tech. Rep. No. 23) (Greensboro, N.C.: Center for Creative Leadership, 1983), p. 34.

[4]Ibid., p. 31.

[5]Quoted in J. P. Kotter, *The General Managers* (New York: Free Press, 1982), p. 17.

[6]H. Mintzberg, D. Raisinghani, and A. Theoret, "The Structure of 'Unstructured' Decision Processes," *Administrative Science Quarterly,* 21, no. 2 (1976), 252.

[7]J. M. Fox, *Executive Qualities* (Reading, Mass.: Addison-Wesley, 1976).

[8]R. Kanter, *Men and Women of the Corporation* (New York: Basic Books, 1977), p. 53.

[9]Thomas, *Medusa and the Snail,* p. 24.

[10]D. Taylor, "Decision Making and Problem Solving," in *Handbook of Organizations,* ed. J. March (Chicago: Rand McNally, 1965), pp. 48–86.

[11]K. D. Fishman, *The Computer Establishment* (New York: Harper & Row, 1981).

[12]Ibid., p. 120.

[13]H. J. Einhorn and R. M. Hogarth, "Decision Making: Going Forward in Reverse," *Harvard Business Review,* 65, no. 1 (1987), 66–70.

[14]Smith, *Corporations in Crisis,* p. 206.

[15]D. Ilgen, C. Fisher, and M. Taylor, "Consequences of Individual Feedback on Behavior in Organizations," *Journal of Applied Psychology,* 64, no. 4 (1979), 349–371.

[16]L. Ross, "The Intuitive Psychologist and His Shortcomings: Distortions in the Attribution Process," in *Advances in Experimental Social Psychology,* Vol, 10, ed. L. Berkowitz (New York: Academic Press, 1977), p. 193.

[17]J. J. Gabarro, "When a New Manager Takes Charge," *Harvard Business Review,* 63, no. 3 (1985), 110–123.

[18]J. G. March and J. P. Olsen, *Ambiguity and Choice in Organizations* (Bergen, Norway: Universitetsforlaget, 1976), p. 20.

[19]P. Mirvis and D. Berg, eds., *Failures in Organization Development and Change* (New York: Wiley, 1977).

[20]Count Philipe-Paul de Segur, *Napoleon's Russian Campaign,* trans. J. David Townsend (Chicago: Time-Life Books, 1958), p. 127.

[21]E. Carter, "The Behavioral Theory of the Firm and Top-Level Corporate Decisions," *Administrative Science Quarterly,* 16, no. 4 (1971), 413–428.

[22]K. Weick, *The Social Psychology of Organizing,* 2nd ed. (Reading, Mass.: Addison-Wesley, 1979).

[23]Attributed to Abraham Lincoln, as cited in W. Manchester, *American Caesar* (New York: Dell, 1978), p. 370.

[24]G. Tuchman, *Making News: A Study in the Construction of Reality* (New York: Free Press, 1978).

[25]D. Whetton, "Organizational Decline: A Neglected Topic in Organizational Science," *Academy of Management Review,* 5, no. 4 (1980), 577–588.

[26]Carter, "Behavioral Theory"; R. Cyert, M. DeGroot, and C. Holt, "Capital Allocation within a Firm," *Behavioral Science,* 24, no. 5 (1979), 287–295.

[27]J. Pfeffer, "The Ambiguity of Leadership," in *Leadership: Where Else Can We Go?* ed. M. W. McCall, Jr. and M. W. Lombardo (Durham, N.C.: Duke University Press, 1978).

[28]J. G. March and Z. Shapira, "Managerial Perspectives on Risk and Risk Taking," *Management Science,* 33, no. 11 (1987), 1414.

[29]H. A. Kissinger, *White House Years* (Boston: Little, Brown, 1979), p. 918.

[30]Fishman, *Computer Establishment,* p. 120.

[31]M. W. McCall, Jr. and M. M. Lombardo, *Off the Track: Why and How Successful Executives Get Derailed* (Tech. Rep. No. 21) (Greensboro, N.C.: Center for Creative Leadership, 1983); M. W. McCall, Jr., M. M. Lombardo, and A. M. Morrison, *The Lessons of Experience* (Lexington, Mass.: Lexington Books, 1988).

[32]March and Shapira, "Managerial Perspectives," p. 1413.

[33]R. E. Kaplan, "An Executive's Reflections on Executives: An Interview with Roger T. Kelley," *Issues and Observations* (Greensboro, N.C.: Center for Creative Leadership, 1982), p. 3.

[34]Smith, *Corporations in Crisis*, p. 19.

[35]J. Tolkien, "The Two Towers," in *Lord of the Rings*, Part 2 (Boston: Houghton Mifflin, 1965), p. 204.

[36]I. I. Mitroff, "Crisis Management: Cutting through the Confusion," *Sloan Management Review*, 29, no. 2 (1988), 15–20.

[37]Kaplan, "Executive's Reflections," p. 3.

[38]Staw and Ross

[39]McCall and Lombardo, *Off the Track*, p. 10.

[40]T. J. Peters and R. H. Waterman, Jr., *In Search of Excellence* (New York: Harper & Row, 1982).

[41]Kanter, *Men and Women*.

[42]J. Newhouse, "A Sporting Game," Part IV, *New Yorker*, July 5, 1982.

[43]Fox, *Executive Qualities*.

[44]Ibid.

# CHAPTER 6

[1]H. Mintzberg, *The Nature of Managerial Work* (New York: Harper & Row, 1973).

[2]J. M. Burns, *Leadership* (New York: Harper & Row, 1978), p. 380.

[3]R. A. Heinlein, *Farnham's Freehold* (New York: Signet, 1964), p. 190.

[4]J. G. March and Z. Shapira, "Managerial Perspectives on Risk and Risk Taking," *Management Science*, 33, no. 11 (1987), 1404–1418.

[5]J. J. Gabarro, *The Dynamics of Taking Charge* (Boston: Harvard Business School Press, 1987); J. P. Kotter, *The General Managers* (New York: Free Press, 1982).

[6]D. A. Schon, *The Reflective Practitioner: How Professionals Think in Action* (New York: Basic Books, 1983); W. R. Torbert, *Managing the Corporate Dream: Restructuring for Long-Term Success* (Homewood, Ill.: Dow Jones-Irwin, 1987).

[7]R. E. Kaplan, W. H. Drath, and J. R. Kofodimos, *High Hurdles: The Challenge of Executive Self-Development* (Greensboro, N.C.: Center for Creative Leadership, 1984).

[8]R. E. Kaplan, *The Expansive Executive* (Greensboro, N.C.: Center for Creative Leadership, 1989).

[9]S. Fink, "A Conversation with Shel Davis," *Exchange*, 4, no. 4 (1979), 17.

[10]D. C. Hambrick and P. A. Mason, "Upper Echelons: The Organization as a Reflection of Its Top Managers," *Academy of Management Review*, 9, no. 2 (1984), 193–206; D. C. Hambrick, "The Top Management Team: Key To Strategic Success," *California Management Review*, 30, no. 1 (1987).

[11]D. J. Isenberg, "Thinking and Managing: A Verbal Protocol Analysis of Managerial Problem Solving," *Academy of Management Journal*, 29, no. 4 (1986), 776.

[12]M. W. McCall, Jr., M. M. Lombardo, and A. M. Morrison, *The Lessons of Experience* (Lexington, Mass.: Lexington Books, 1988).

[13]S. Kerr, "On the Folly of Rewarding A, While Hoping for B," *Academy of Management Journal*, 18, no. 4 (1975), 769–783.

[14]T. J. Peters and R. H. Waterman, Jr., *In Search of Excellence* (New York: Harper & Row, 1982).

[15]R. H. Hayes, "Why Strategic Planning Goes Awry," *New York Times,* April 20, 1986, sec. 3, p. 2; H. Mintzberg, "Crafting Strategy," *Harvard Business Review,* 65, no. 4 (1987), 66–75.

[16]McCall, Lombardo, and Morrison, *Lessons of Experience.*

[17]Peters and Waterman, *In Search of Excellence.*

[18]Kotter, *General Managers.*

# *INDEX*

## A

Accidents, and problem priorities, 52–53
Action, 109
  foundation for in managers, 66–67
  manager's learning from, 87
  moving from priorities to (*figure*), 87
  quick vs. convoluted, 66–85
  thoughtful, 116–117
Action outcomes, rules for negotiating perception
    of, 101–107
Action, convoluted, 62–63, 73–85
  advantages of, 77
  characteristics of, 76–77
  complexity of, 73–77
  and delays (example), 78–79
  drawbacks of, 77
  elements of, 77–84
  and image of progress, 83
  involvement of many people, 77
  kinds of decisions requiring, 77–78
  major interruptions in, 76
  and manager's bargaining tactics, 81
  and manager's personal contacts, 83–84
  need for champion, 79–81
  relation to quick action, 85
  rules for, 84–85
  struggle in, 89

and strategic decision model (*figure*), 75
  time required for, 76
Action, quick, 67–73
  advantages of, 69
  and business turnaround, 72
  characteristics of, 67–70
  and commitment to failing project, 69
  and crisis management, 71
  disadvantages of, 69–70
  as fact of organizational life, 68
  and lack of valuable dissent, 70
  and problem dissection, 71–72
  relation to convoluted action, 85
  and research on managers, 67
  and risk assessment, 72
  rules for, 73
  and unexpected events, 70–71
  and unilateral decision making, 67
Activities, manager's and problems faced, 40
Agenda setting, 44
Agendas:
  as controllable by manager, 114
  created by manager, 58–59
  and general managers, 59
Allied attack through Holland, 4
Ambiguity of decision consequences, 92–
    96
Ambition, and withholding of information, 19
Anticipation, and decision-making, 56

# F

# G

# H

# E

## I

## J

## K

## L

## M

## W

## X